SOCIAL ANALYSIS

Linking Faith and Justice

Revised and Enlarged Edition

JOE HOLLAND
PETER HENRIOT, S.J.

DOVE COMMUNICATIONS and
ORBIS BOOKS
in collaboration with
THE CENTER OF CONCERN

Nineteenth Printing, February 2004

The Catholic Foreign Mission Society of America (Maryknoll) recruits and trains people for overseas missionary service. Through Orbis Books Maryknoll aims to foster the international dialogue that is essential to mission. The books published, however, reflect the opinions of their authors and are not meant to represent the official position of the society.

Library of Congress Cataloging in Publication Data

Holland, Joe.
  Social analysis.

  Bibliography: p.
  1. Church and social problems—Catholic Church.
2. Social justice. 3. Social change. I. Henriot,
Peter. II. Title.
HN37.C3H583 1983   261.8'3   83-6259

Revised and enlarged edition published in Australia in 1983 by Dove Communications, Box 316, Blackburn, Victoria 3130, Australia

Dove ISBN: 0-859-24-263-3

For William F. Ryan, S.J.,
Founding Director, Center of Concern, 1971–1977,
whose strong leadership, friendship, and support
have helped us link faith and justice

Contents

SOCIAL ANALYSIS

It is up to Christian communities to analyze with objectivity the situation which is proper to their own country, to shed on it the light of the Gospel's unalterable words, and to draw principles of reflections, norms of judgment, and directives of action from the social teaching of the Church.

Octogesima Adveniens, No. 4

Foreword

In the Autumn of 1980, we published the first edition of *Social Analysis: Linking Faith and Justice*. The response has been dramatic.

Over 45,000 copies have been distributed in two years from the Center of Concern. In England, the Catholic Institute for International Relations distributed 2,500 copies to its subscribers. In addition, there has been a separate Asian English edition published in the Philippines (3,500 copies), a French edition published in Montreal, and large sections translated into Spanish for use in Latin America, as well as into Japanese and Chinese. There are also translations of Section 2 into several African languages.

Besides the written word, we prepared this past year a four-part video cassette series, which has enjoyed great popularity in the United States.

All of the staff of the Center of Concern have been asked to present workshops and seminars on the theme of social analysis. This has taken us to colleges, dioceses, religious congregations, and conventions throughout the United States. We have also travelled to Canada, the Philippines, Hong Kong, Zambia, Zimbabwe, Rome, Ireland, England, Mexico, and Colombia, responding to invitations for seminars on social analysis.

Our material has been picked up and used by many others—in newsletters, books, courses, workshops, and in countless other ways.

After several reprintings of the first edition of *Social Analysis,* we decided to prepare a second edition. We do this for two reasons. First, this provides us an opportunity to offer further reflections by way of a newly-written "Preface" and "Afterword." Second, we can present the text in a more durable version.

The "Preface," written by Joe Holland, situates the task of social analysis within a wider understanding of the crisis of modern civilization. By concentrating on the meaning of "root metaphors," Joe probes some of the subsequent reflections which have come out of our social analysis work. In particular, he discusses the relationship between social analysis, theological reflection, and spirituality.

Peter Henriot presents in the "Afterword" a practical methodology for doing social analysis at the local level. This topic was repeatedly requested of us after the first edition of our book, as readers sought some concrete guidance for applying social analysis in their immediate environment. Peter also outlines some approaches to the theological reflection called for by the "pastoral circle."

Two words about the "pastoral circle." First, the role of *experience* is primary. But obviously we are not speaking about "raw" experience, as if we have access to something that exists in a vacuum, unrelated to the interpretations we place upon it. Experience is fundamental, but always mediated. In order to clarify this important point, we have in this second edition redesigned the pastoral circle to show that the four moments, or elements, of our approach are all mediations of experience. The first moment, then, we have called "insertion," the lively contact with the experienced reality which is being analyzed.

Second, the four elements—insertion, social analysis, theological reflection, and pastoral planning—all need to be located in an atmosphere of celebration, infused with an ethos of prayer. This provides a time of discernment, openness, liturgy, song and music. It means that the more intellectual elements of analysis, reflection, and planning are continually grounded in experience. Celebration and prayer make the pastoral circle genuinely human and spirit-filled and give the struggle for linking faith and justice new meaning, new life.

Many people have contributed to the development of *Social Analysis*. We owe much to our colleagues at the Center of Concern for their continuous support, helpful suggestions, and invaluable insights. We appreciate the editorial assistance of Jane Blewett and Elizabeth Schmidt and the long hours of typing of many drafts by Anne Stygles and Lucinda Williams. Thousands of people in the United States and other countries have, by their lively participation in our workshops, sharpened our own understanding of the meaning and application of social analysis. And we are especially grateful for our benefactors, whose encouragement, prayers, and large and small contributions make possible our life at the Center of Concern.

Joe Holland
Peter Henriot, S.J.

Preface

by Joe Holland

In the few short years since helping to write *Social Analysis,* I find that my thinking on our social crisis grows ever more radical. By "radical" I mean going to the root of the question. Specifically, my focus has shifted from "society" to "civilization." In the first edition of this book, the focus was on the social crisis of advanced industrial capitalism. I would now argue that *our whole Western civilization has entered into a profound and irreversible crisis.*

The words "society" and "civilization" are of course both wide-ranging, but "civilization" runs deeper. The term "society" came to dominance with the modern "social question" and the rise of the modern social sciences. It focuses on economics and politics. The term "civilization," by contrast, belongs more to a deeper tradition in the West. "Civilization" connotes greater emphasis on culture, and, within culture, on religion. It is this *question of culture, and within it religion, which reveals, I believe, the most radical dimension of our social crisis.*

This may sound strange, for our book *Social Analysis* focuses primarily on economics and on politics. Is this then a rejection of that approach? I don't think so. Rather it is a deepening.

It is true that within industrial capitalism, which is analyzed in this book, economic life largely shapes political and cultural life. But is that all there is to say? Are there not still deeper questions? For example, was the emergence of an industrial capitalism, where economics is largely determining, itself to be explained by economics? Or is there perhaps a deeper cultural key? Still further, is the transformation of an economically determined social system to occur simply by economic drives or political forces? Or is there again a deeper cultural key? To these questions, both of the roots and of the transformation of industrial capitalism, I believe culture is basic.

This is not to deny that culture arises from and is shaped by its economic and political context. Of course it is, and it cannot be understood except as embodied in such a context. Culture is never an angelic spirit floating above society.

But it is the other extreme to conceive culture simply as the prisoner of its context, or the mere reflection of economic drives and political forces, or only an ideological justification for social structures. Certainly culture often functions in the mode of legitimation, but it can also be the point of critique and creativity. Again this critique and creativity always have a social base, but the energy which flows from them has still deeper roots.

The deepest source of cultural energies, indeed the deepest source of all human creativity, flows from *participation in divine creativity*. The creativity of human culture is humanity's participation in the creative Spirit of God who brooded over the waters in Genesis and still moves within the depths of human civilization.

But in the crisis of our present civilization these energies of creativity are being converted on a massive scale into energies of destruction.

Crisis of Civilization

Increasingly the energies of our civilization are pointed toward destruction—toward destruction of the poor, toward destruction of those who speak for life and justice, toward destruction of family and community, toward destruction of our precious earth, toward destruction of the human race. At their root, these energies of destruction are extinguishing the image of God in humanity and in all of creation. They become demonic.

The classical analyses of the secular Left and the religious Right break down before this cultural crisis of all industrial civilization. (Industrial civilization is a more comprehensive concept than industrial capitalism, although industrial capitalism is at its heart.)

The *classic secular Left* has rightly perceived the great drive toward social destruction at the heart of modern civilization. But it has generally failed to perceive the destructive blocking of divine creativity, which flows from an ever-deepening "progressive" secularization of society. The classic Left thus challenges social destruction, but cuts itself off from the religious root of creativity.

As a result, its efforts to stop the destruction often prove sterile, and sometimes even compound the crisis. The flat vision of secular scientific socialism, or of a secular scientific state as the key to the future, feeds the loss of cultural creativity.

The situation on the *classic religious Right* is just the opposite, with the same unfortunate result. For the religious Right, the main problem is secularization. It correctly sees the whole "progressive" movement as deepening secularization and therefore cutting itself off from the divine root. But the religious Right fails to understand the prophetic side of the divine, and winds up defending the very social destruction that the Left fights against.

The Right tries to retrieve an authoritarian, patriarchal, militaristic society tied this time to powerful modern technology. It appeals to a divine image, but that divine image is no longer the living God of justice and peace. It is rather a war god, a god of oppression, an idol. This idol in turn provides religious legitimation for demonic destruction.

Thus on one side the secular Left often makes of secularization its own idol and cuts itself off from the divine root of human creativity. On the other side, the religious Right holds high the principle of religious transcendence, but often allows a false god to unleash the demonic.

The complete task is to link faith energies with energies of justice and peace in service of the Living God and social transformation. Faith and justice need to become as one flesh in service of both. The secular hunger for justice from the Left needs to find its deeper root in spirituality. The spiritual hunger of the Right needs to find God's true face in justice and peace.

There are two seeds of creativity in the world—social engagement and spirituality. Similarly within the Christian community, these two movements have their echo—on one side the justice and peace movement, often developed in a secular style; and on the other side the prayer movement, often without social engagement.

It is sad when good people from both sides fail to see the other's complementary gift. It is sad when some from the justice and peace movement are uneasy with the powerful explosion of spiritual energies from the charismatic and evangelical movements.[1] Do they fail to understand the spontaneity of religious energies? Similarly it is sad when some from the prayer movement develop analyses and alliances aimed at fighting the justice and peace movement.[2] Do they fail to understand the prophetic call of God?

Is it the terrible sin of human pride on both sides which causes this division? Is it the pride of secularism on the Left—afraid of spiritual energies because they are not subject to rational control? And is it the pride of religiosity on the Right—afraid of the Spirit's prophetic power in the secular arena because it is not subject to religious control?

Fortunately, there are positive signs of healing and merger. Liberation theology, for example, represents a re-rooting of the secularized prophetic sense of the Left back into its religious source.[3] Similarly we see new outreaches from charismatics and evangelicals toward prophetic social engagement.[4] Both these sources of energies are needed to face the deepening destructiveness of our industrial civilization.

Thus we may speak of *two criteria* for guiding our path in the crisis which envelops us. The first criterion is *openness to the creative transformation of our civilization.* The second criterion is *openness to the spiritual roots of creative energies.* The classic secular Left fails the test of the second criterion. The classic religious Right fails the test of the first criterion.

Both criteria are needed to challenge industrial capitalism, and more widely the whole of industrial civilization, including its extension into industrial communism.

Industrial capitalism, based in Western Europe and North America, has marginalized religious energies and tried to crush their prophetic face, even while honoring religion. This has resulted in a destructive industrial civilization whose cultural-spiritual roots are everyday withering, and which threatens vast destruction.

Industrial communism, based in the Soviet Union and Eastern

Europe, has tried to eliminate religious energies in a scientific society, but it treads the same destructive path as industrial capitalism. Indeed, one might argue, both industrial capitalism and industrial communism are entering into negative convergence in the single social and spiritual crisis of industrial civilization. Both industrial capitalism and industrial communism are struggling to shape the destiny of the Third World, but there we see new signs of social and spiritual creativity which transcend both. This is particularly true with the church.

Root Metaphors and Culture

The move toward this wider and deeper perspective shared here has two main sources, which it might be helpful to report on briefly. The first is the recent work of Gibson Winter around the question of the "root metaphors" which shape civilizations. The second is the social and religious reflection of Pope John Paul II on the crisis of modern Western civilization.

Gibson Winter, a professor of social ethics at Princeton University, has drawn attention to the *mechanistic root metaphor at the cultural foundation of modern civilization.*[5] In other places, I have tried to summarize and elaborate on Gibson Winter's insights, especially as they provide a mediating instrument to link social analysis and theological reflection.[6] But here let me offer a brief summary.

In essence, since the rise of modern autonomous science, whether mediated through the free market of the capitalist system or the centralized state of the communist system, or a combination of both, industrial civilization has been constructing itself in the model of *the machine.* This model flows from the thinking of seminal figures like Bacon, Newton, Descartes, Locke, Hobbes, etc.

Ideally the mechanistic drive in society sought to free humanity from its chains to nature and tradition. But the drive of the machine has now become all-consuming. It is dissolving the civilization's spiritual depth. It is converting people into objects. And its energies, without rhythm or rest, are increasingly destructive. Designed to free humanity, the mechanistic society is now trying to make humanity and the earth into its slave, and then move to destroy both.

Over against this mechanistic root metaphor, at the cultural foundation of modern imagination, Gibson Winter proposes that a new root metaphor is emerging as an antidote to protect the preciousness of humanity and the earth. It is the *artistic root metaphor*. Rather than seeing society as a scientific machine, it proposes a vision of society as a *work of art,* flowing from the creativity of rooted communities in solidarity with each other. The crisis of our civilization is precisely a struggle for which root metaphor will shape our cultural imagination—an increasingly destructive mechanistic one, or an emerging creative artistic one.

All kinds of social and religious consequences flow from this conflict of visions, but there is not space here to develop them. Yet I might just propose a basic social and religious principle flowing from this new root metaphor, namely *the social and spiritual creativity of rooted communities networked in solidarity*.

Similar lines of analysis are developed by Pope John Paul II in his encyclicals, speeches, and other writings.[7] Again there is not space here to develop or cite his thought in any detail, so I will just lay out what seems to be the essence of it.

People on the Left are sometimes critical of the pope's thought. Indeed on certain themes, especially bearing on women, role models, and clericalism in the church, he seems partly a prisoner of his traditional past. But in his wider social analysis of militarism, unions, human rights, and the role of faith in the modern world, I believe he is one of the most original and powerful thinkers of post-modern times.

Basically, the pope argues that we have come to an *inescapable crisis of modern civilization*. There are two sides to this crisis.

On the negative side, if its destructive energies are allowed to continue, they will destroy humanity and the earth. Thus he constantly refers to the danger of slow destruction by ecological contamination or rapid destruction by nuclear holocaust. These same destructive tendencies are played out in the death of the unborn, the oppression of labor, the abandonment of the poor, the collapse of the family, and the massive world-wide violations of human rights, especially through torture.

On the positive side, new energies are emerging to create a fresh civilization. The pope does not refer to this in traditional Catholic terms as "Christian civilization," but rather as a broader "civilization of love."

Basically, to overcome the destructive crisis of modern civilization, the pope argues, we need to create a new civilization based on human dignity and cooperative solidarity. This means new economic and political institutions and a new cultural foundation.

Industrial capitalism is clearly wrong, for it has put capital over labor and thus inverted the basic structure of human dignity, leaving labor as an economic victim.

Industrial communism rightfully protested against this inversion, but failed to change it. Instead it simply placed capital in the hands of a centralized state, and left labor as its political victim.

The key economic and political task is to restore the primacy of labor over capital by means of workers' self-management and cooperatives, with the state as their servant in an open, participatory model. But to move toward this solution, we need to go deeper than economics and politics, to the cultural foundations.

Culture for Pope John Paul II is the deeper key. Buried within the cultural foundations of modern civilization is a basic flaw. It has both a religious and social expression. The religious expression is negative—the culture has lost contact with its spiritual roots. The social expression is also negative—it is turning against humanity. Both expressions are inextricably bound together. Our path back to healing is via the human, but through the human to the divine. *Humanism and theism are not antagonistic, but complementary.* The human is not safeguarded without its foundation in the divine, and the divine is not accessible except through the human.

But modern civilization, which has produced two sequential forms of ideology, first industrial capitalism and then, in reaction, industrial communism, now finds that these ideologies are exhausting their energies. The deepest answer is not in liberating the free market, although economic creativity remains important. Nor is the deepest answer in state-centered politicization, though politics is central to the task. Rather the deepest answer is in a new cultural vision.

Deeper Vision

What is the nature of this new civilization struggling to be born? Some would call it a communitarian socialism, others simply a communitarian society. Many have pointed out the ecological and feminist principles as foundational. Certainly it needs to be grounded on a vision which begins with the poor. And finally the analysis suggests it will be a more explicitly religious civilization, not setting the spiritual against the material, but discovering that the material world is indeed spirit-filled. This question of the nature of the new civilization needs to become one of our most important social and religious challenges. Again, culture, even more than economics or politics (but never in isolation from them), may be the key to the vision.

Both Gibson Winter and Pope John Paul II call us to this deeper cultural vision. The vision does not repudiate what we have offered here in *Social Analysis*. Indeed insofar as human experience is the path, this book is an important step toward that deeper vision. But it is only a step. The deeper task of cultural and spiritual analysis still lies before us.

But again, this task needs social roots. For that reason, I believe the most important single step we can take is to begin *to root our cultural analysis and theological reflection within the life of those who make up the mainstream of the Christian community, namely the laity.*

"Laity" is, however, a misleading word. We often use it in the sense of amateur, as opposed to specialist. Most of us understand ourselves as lay people in the field of health, yielding to the scientific mystique of the medical priesthood. So too in the field of religion, we normally condense religious competence into the clergy or, more widely, religious professionals. But "laity" has an older root meaning, in the sense of the Greek *laos* or "people." The laity of the church is the *People of God,* including all Christians.

In our increasingly technical and professional culture (with roots in the clerical Middle Ages), we have so differentiated the professional from the common people as even to set professionals antagonistically over against the people. Medical doctors for example have become a new priesthood, failing to provide broad popular education in preventative medicine and thereby creating a professional monopolization of skills which rewards them financially but injures society. The same thing has happened in the religious field where the more we have professionalized our ministries, the more uprooted they have become.

Unfortunately this is even the case in the justice and peace movement in the church, and perhaps especially there. Neoconservative critics speak disparagingly of a "new class" of manipulative professionals who increase their control over various social institutions by monopolizing information and skills in a particular area. Something of this seems to have happened in the church as well. The justice and peace movement, at least in our own country, has often neglected the wider People of God, often disparaged the parish system, and at the extreme sometimes seen Christians of "middle class" as the enemy.

Fortunately that has changed some in recent years. There is the beginning of a new lay and parish-based tone to the justice and peace movement.[8] But it cannot expand quickly enough.

To help this change, we are gifted with a new model of church coming especially from the Third World, namely, the *basic Christian community*. The formation of small lay communities, mainly within the parish structure, is the key to re-rooting the movement for justice and peace at the base. This is not the place to give practical instructions about basic communities, but I wish to call attention to their importance here.

Some have argued that basic communities are good for the South of the globe, but not for the North. Perhaps their argument is founded on a misunderstanding of the phenomenon. I would judge that there is a great hunger for basic communities across the church of the North, and that they are constantly emerging with other names. The small communities which gather for Christian Family Movement, for charismatic prayer, for programs like "RENEW" and "Ashes to Easter," for "Marriage Encounter," for the "Cursillo," and for countless other movements, are often founded on this very hunger for small, faith-filled community. Indeed *the hunger for community is perhaps one of the most important pastoral indicators in a society so marked by rootlessness, fragmentation, and spiritual sterility.*

But our task in the industrial West may be even more difficult in that regard than in the Third World. There in many cases the traditional foundations of community and spirituality are still strong. Here they have often been eroded. There it may be more a matter of communities deepening their religious and social root. Here we often need instead to replant the social and religious seeds for community.

I would also make a *special plea to the religious orders of the Catholic church to find new ways of bonding with the laity*—not to remove the laity from their roots, but to be of better service to them. I believe this will mean new models of lay membership, as equals and peers of those with the traditional vows, and perhaps even new explicitly lay forms of the religious order.

There was a time when the religious orders of necessity separated themselves from the local church in order to pursue their prophetic witness through the vows in a separate state of life. We spoke of this as "leaving the world." But now, as the whole church is called to become prophetic, it is the task of the religious orders precisely to bond with the local church in order to nourish the prophetic vocation of all Christians.

In conclusion, if social analysis is to take on power, it needs on one side to turn to culture and its creative spiritual roots, and on the other side to root itself in the experience and discernment of small communities of lay Christians at the base of the church. The most important prophetic and pastoral task before us, therefore, is the gathering of these communities, under lay leadership, to face the social and spiritual forces of our foundational cultural crisis.

NOTES

1. I frequently hear this fear articulated by friends in the Catholic justice and peace networks.

2. An example of this fear, it seems to me, is Ralph Martin's book *The Crisis of Truth* (Ann Arbor, Mich.: Servant Books, 1982). Contrast it with another evangelically flavored book, but more engaging with the social question, namely Jim Wallis's *Call to Conversion* (San Francisco: Harper & Row, 1981).

3. Liberation theology is often criticized for being Marxist. Arthur McGovern in *Marxism: An American Christian Perspective* (Maryknoll, N.Y.: Orbis Books, 1980) takes the position that the main lines of liberation theology are not Marxist, but rather biblical and Catholic. I would describe it as post-Marxist, indeed post-modern, but that is a matter for another essay.

4. See Dom Helder Camara and Cardinal Suenens' book, *Charismatic Renewal and Social Action: A Dialogue* (Ann Arbor, Mich.: Ser-

vant Books, 1979). See also evangelical publications like *Sojourners* (Washington, D.C.) and *The Other Side* (Philadelphia).

5. Gibson Winter, *Liberating Creation: Foundations of Religious Social Ethics* (New York: Crossroad, 1981).

6. See my essay in the volume on theological reflection from the Woodstock Theological Center at Georgetown University, edited by James Hug, *Tracing the Spirit: Communities, Social Action, and Theological Reflection* (New York: Paulist Press, 1983).

7. The pope's three encyclicals are *Redemptor Hominis,* March 4, 1979, *Dives in Misericordia,* December 7, 1980, and *Laborem Exercens,* September 15, 1981. See also his address to the 68th session of the International Labor Organization, June 15, 1982, titled, "Human Labor and the Requirements of Solidarity." Another helpful text is his earlier book *Sign of Contradiction* (London: Hodder and Staughton, 1979).

8. To my mind, one of the most exciting developments is the attempt to draw whole families into the justice and peace movement. See, for example, the work of Kathy and Jim McGinnis in the National Parenting for Peace and Justice Network and their book *Parenting for Peace and Justice* (Maryknoll, N.Y.: Orbis Books, 1981).

Introduction

How we see a problem determines how we respond to it. Is this true? Suppose for a moment that you, the reader of this study, are planning some pastoral response to a particular issue that confronts you. You want to make the best response possible. How do you see the issue?

A. You are in charge of a regional program relating to the hunger issue. In order to achieve the program's goal of educating people to the problem of world hunger and helping them to respond with action, you face a decision regarding priorities for the coming year.

On the one hand, you can focus on the shocking statistics of 800 million malnourished people around the world and the grim prospects for producing and distributing an adequate supply of food in the 1980s. You can describe the gap between rich and poor countries and speak of the waste for which we, in the United States, are responsible each day. Finally, you can urge people to donate money to the various relief services that feed the hungry.

Or, on the other hand, you can point to the structural causes of hunger, linking hunger to poverty. You can show how the activities of multinational agribusiness corporations, the trade and foreign aid policies of the United States government, and the autocratic rule of certain Third World elites have kept the majority of people impoverished and hungry. You can research links between poverty in the U.S. and poverty in developing countries, demonstrating the similarity of the factors involved, e.g., land tenure, ownership of productive means, employment, etc. Finally, you can involve people in efforts to reform U.S. foreign aid policies and to improve the domestic food stamp program, so that in neither case will people be kept in dependency relationships.

B. You are the coordinator of educational resources for a large religious congregation that has worked for years in a midwestern city. You staff several schools in the inner-city area, and you are faced with a decision regarding personnel allocations. In one specific school, for example, you can: (1) remove teachers from the school (effectively shutting down its operation); (2) keep the same number of staff working there; or (3) increase the staff. How do you reach the decision?

On the one hand, you can simply look at the decision as a matter for popular vote within the congregation and ask that the members be polled for their opinions. You know that there are strong feelings regarding all three options, and you want to avoid a lot of lengthy discussions. So you let the majority opinion determine the direction of your pastoral response.

Or, on the other hand, you can study the racial and ethnic character of the neighborhood and determine what future is projected for it in terms of overall urban development. You can ask what other educational opportunities are available in the area and what impact quality education may have on family stability, rate of employment, and community potential for change. You can listen to the desires of local leaders regarding the future of the area and the possibility of community control over educational institutions. Finally, you can look at the number of personnel at your disposal, weighing the fact that the median age of your congregation is advancing markedly each year. Only with this broad picture would you attempt to reach a decision, by popular vote or in any other fashion.

C. You are the director of a community organization working to improve the housing conditions in an old northeastern city. The community organization is faced with the fact that middle- and upper-income people are returning to inner-city neighborhoods, displacing poor minority families from inexpensive housing. You must make a decision regarding the selection of focal issues around which to rally people in order to most effectively preserve housing opportunities for the poor.

On the one hand, you can survey the situation and simply pick whatever issue is most immediate and well-known. For instance, you hear talk about a few realtors who obviously are "making a killing" in their promotion of the "gentrification" process, realtors who don't even live in the neighborhood. You decide to lead demonstrations in front of their offices to publicize their actions.

Or, on the other hand, you can study the overall housing plan for the city and region, determining long-term trends and needs. You can identify the key economic factors influencing the return to the city—e.g., the energy crisis, new job opportunities for professionals, a shift in mortgage rates by local banks, etc. You learn that there are no laws restricting the rate at which apartment houses can be converted into condominiums, and you see the need for a special "speculation tax" that would take the profit out of spiraling real estate speculation. Finally, after making a careful study of the situation, you can encourage local churches and synagogues to institute alternative investment programs, making more money available to the community, specifically, in housing cooperatives for the poor.

Obviously, in the real world, these simple "either/or" choices would not offer themselves in such a clearcut fashion. There is considerable overlap in decisions that face us, and our responses may be of a very mixed character.

But recall the point we are making here: how we see the problem determines how we respond to it. In the second response to each of the above problems, deeper structural issues were explored, causal linkages examined, key factors identified, long-term trends traced. The *ad hoc,* more immediate actions of the first responses were chosen without deeper study, on the basis of minimal information about more systemic issues. What characterizes the second responses, in contrast to the first responses, is an effort to see the wider picture and to initiate action that affects more profound social change. This "seeing a wider picture" is the result of *social analysis*. As a tool of pastoral action, social analysis is an integral part of the ministry for social justice.

OUR APPROACH

In the pages that follow, we will be exploring the meaning of "social analysis" and its relevance to action on behalf of justice. In recent years, so much attention has focused on the topic of social analysis—by community activists, educators, religious groups, organizations concerned with Third World issues, feminist groups, etc.—that the Center of Concern felt a brief and uncomplicated study on the topic would be helpful for many people.

The purpose of this study is simple: to describe the task of social analysis and its relevance to social justice action, to provide illustrations of analytical approaches to various problems, and to explore the suggestions and questions they raise for pastoral responses.

- *Chapter 1* **answers the question, what is the meaning of "social analysis"? It briefly describes the history of the current interest in the topic, explores the problems that arise when individuals try to utilize social analysis, and examines the various elements of the social analytic approach.**
- *Chapter 2* **discusses various interpretations of the process of social change and shows different approaches to social action in response to the various analytic models.**
- *Chapter 3* **considers the topic of international development and its implications for social justice action. It analyzes three models of development and the consequences of each for political and pastoral responses on both the international and domestic levels.**
- *Chapter 4* **suggests an analytic approach to understanding various pastoral responses to the process of industrialization and raises questions for future pastoral action.**

We conclude the study with some remarks about the "limits" to social analysis and suggestions for persons or groups interested in using it on the local level.

Our study has several characteristics that should be stated at the outset:

First, the study is a "working paper," not a final and definitive analysis. We are offering an introduction to social analysis, not in formal textbook fashion, but through an informal discussion of what we perceive to be its elements and implications.

Second, we do not offer a simple "how to" approach to social analysis, a manual of "ten easy steps" for application to your local situation. Rather, we explore the development of the new interest in social analysis and demonstrate its usefulness in approaching social justice action. As a tool of pastoral action, social analysis should not be accepted uncritically, but should itself be subjected to probing examination.

Third, we do not shy away from certain controversial critiques or provocative positions. We hope to stimulate reactions—disagreements as well as agreements—that will complement our efforts and expand our horizons.

Fourth, the study is written from a particular perspective and reveals the biases of the authors. It is *not* "value-free." Our perspective is influenced by an explicitly Christian commitment to gospel values, enlightened by the heritage of the social teaching of the church. Moreover, we write from a U.S. base, although our perspective is strongly influenced by a global view and an international stance.

Our biases also include:

- **Belief that pastoral action necessarily includes action on behalf of justice.**
- **Rejection of sharp dichotomies between "sacred and secular," "religious and political," "this world and the world to come," "development and evangelization."**
- **Acceptance of the integral link between the service of faith and the promotion of justice.**
- **Option for the poor, with consequent entry into social reality *"desde los pobres"*—from the side of the poor.**
- **Commitment to social change through change of structures, in addition to personal and interpersonal conversion.**
- **Affirmation of the proper role for value discussion in public discourse, e.g., human questions in economic policy debates.**
- **Concern that the current course of events—"business as usual"—is leading the United States and the world toward imminent disaster.**

We emphasize the perspectives and biases of our study because we feel strongly that the type of social analysis needed for pastoral action today should be heavily value-laden. Frankly, we are suspicious of any analysis—from the Left, the Center, or the Right—that purports a "scientific objectivity" about its study of reality. We choose to acknowledge our values and admit that they influence our choice of topics, manner of approach, and character of response.

In this study, oriented toward pastoral action on behalf of social justice, we consider social analysis a primary tool for linking faith and justice. If faith is to be alive in the works of justice, then the reality of the social situation must be clearly understood. Social analysis moves us toward that understanding.

Chapter 1

Social Analysis: Tool of Pastoral Action

There can be two approaches to social analysis. Let's call one "academic" and the other "pastoral." The academic approach studies a particular social situation in a detached, fairly abstract manner, dissecting its elements for the purpose of understanding. The pastoral approach, on the other hand, looks at the reality from an involved, historically committed stance, discerning the situation for the purpose of action.

This "academic" vs. "pastoral" dichotomy is, of course, overdrawn in order to emphasize the differences. One can be "academic," in the sense of a scholarly pursuit of knowledge, yet at the same time be committed to social action. However, social analysis, as it is treated in this essay, is not simply an exercise in scholarship. Rather, it is analysis in the service of action for justice. It is an integral part of "the faith that does justice."

THE PASTORAL CIRCLE

A social analysis that is genuinely pastoral can be illustrated in what we can call the "pastoral circle." This circle represents the close relationships between four mediations of experience: (1) *insertion,* (2) *social analysis,* (3) *theological reflection,* and (4) *pastoral planning* (see Diagram I, p. 8)

DIAGRAM I
THE PASTORAL CIRCLE

This circle is frequently referred to as the "circle of praxis," because it emphasizes the on-going relationship between reflection and action. (The concept of *praxis* has been developed by Paulo Freire in his classic, *The Pedagogy of the Oppressed*, New York: Herder and Herder, 1970.) It is related to what has been called the "hermeneutic circle," or the method of interpretation that sees new questions continually raised to challenge older theories by the force of new situations. (This method is explored in Juan Luis Segundo's, *The Liberation of Theology*, Maryknoll, N.Y.: Orbis Books, 1976.)

The first moment in the pastoral circle—and the basis for any pastoral action—is *insertion*. This locates the geography of our pastoral responses in the lived experience of individuals and communities. What people are feeling, what they are undergoing, how they are responding—these are the experiences that constitute primary data. We gain access to these by inserting our approach close to the experiences of ordinary people.

These experiences must be understood in the richness of all their interrelationships. This is the task of *social analysis*, the second moment in the pastoral circle. Social analysis examines causes, probes consequences, delineates linkages, and identifies actors. It helps make sense of experiences by putting them into a broader picture and drawing the connections between them.

The third moment is *theological reflection*, an effort to understand more broadly and deeply the analyzed experience in the light of living faith, scripture, church social teaching, and the resources of tradition. The Word of God brought to bear upon the situation raises new questions, suggests new insights, and opens new responses.

Since the purpose of the pastoral circle is decision and action, the fourth moment in the circle is crucial: *pastoral planning*. In the light of experiences analyzed and reflected upon, what response is called for by individuals and by communities? How should the response be designed in order to be most effective not only in the short term but also in the long term?

A response of action in a particular situation brings about a situation of new experiences. These experiences in turn call for further mediation through insertion, analysis, reflection, and planning. Thus, the pastoral circle continues without final conclusion. It is, in fact, more of a "spiral" than a "circle." Each approach does not simply retrace old steps but breaks new grounds.

Key Questions

Before moving on, it is important to note that each of these moments in the pastoral circle should themselves be subjected to critical examination. When pastoral action on behalf of justice is the goal for which we are striving, then the following questions must be asked:

1. *Insertion*—Where and with whom are we locating ourselves as we begin our process? Whose experience is being considered? Are there groups that are "left out" when experience is discussed? Does the experience of the poor and oppressed have a privileged role to play in the process?

2. *Social Analysis*—Which analytical tradition is being followed? Are there presuppositions in these analyses that need to be tested? Is it possible to use a particular analysis without agreeing with its accompanying ideology?

3. *Theological Reflection*—What methodological assumptions underlie the theological reflection? In what relationship does the

social analysis stand to the theology—e.g., complementary, subordinate, etc.? How closely linked is the theology to the existing social situation?

4. *Pastoral planning*—Who participates in the pastoral planning? What are the implications of the process used to determine appropriate responses? What is the relationship between groups who serve and those who are served?

We hope to elaborate on these questions throughout the study—opening the debate, but not claiming to give final answers.

Beyond Anecdotes

Our discussion of the pastoral circle will be recognized by many who are familiar with the "see/judge/act" trilogy of Canon Joseph Cardijn, the Belgian priest who, prior to World War II, inspired Catholic social action groups such as the Young Christian Workers, Young Christian Students, and, indirectly, the Christian Family Movement. When Cardijn urged social activists to "see," he called upon them to do more than simply *look* at the facts and figures of a particular situation. Beyond these facts and figures lies a framework that provides meaning, a perspective that makes sense of disparate elements. The search for this framework is the task of social analysis.

Effective pastoral planning necessarily involves this movement *from the anecdotal to the analytical*. We must move from issues— e.g., the high cost of housing, job discrimination against non-whites, the decline of urban services, exclusion of women in decision-making posts, hunger in developing countries, etc.— to explanations of *why* things are the way they are. To stop with anecdotes, to concentrate only on issues, obscures the comprehensive systemic picture. If the picture is obscured, one becomes trapped in immediate, *ad hoc* solutions.

Social problems and issues, although they may appear to be isolated pieces, are actually linked together in a larger system. Consider, for example, the huge woven tapestries that adorn the walls of many religious houses and art museums. These tapestries—intricate mazes of thousands of connected threads—tell elaborate stories of saints, soldiers, and statesmen. If we were to step behind these old tapestries, we could see that the threads are woven back and forth, linking individual elements of the total picture. If someone were to pull at these threads, the various pieces of the picture would move in a variety of directions throughout the tapestry.

Social analysis attempts to provide a similar sense of the systemic unity of reality. Within the context of social analysis, facts and issues are no longer regarded as isolated problems. Rather, they are perceived as interrelated parts of a whole. Using social analysis, we can respond to that larger picture in a more systematic fashion. By dealing with the whole, rather than with detached parts, we are able to move beyond "issue orientation," or a primarily pragmatic approach, toward a holistic or systemic approach.

Calls for Analysis

The church has increasingly recognized that social analysis is important for effective pastoral planning. In his 1971 social document, "A Call to Action" (*Octogesima adveniens*), Pope Paul VI challenged social activists in a manner that recalls the elements of the pastoral circle:

It is up to Christian communities to analyze with objectivity the situation which is proper to their own country, to shed on it the light of the Gospel's unalterable words, and to draw principles or reflections, norms of judgment, and directives of action from the social teaching of the Church [No. 4].

This call came into the life of one international religious community and was recorded in the 1975 documents of the 32nd General Congregation of the Society of Jesus. In its Decree Four, "Our Mission Today," the Jesuit mission is described as an integral approach to "the service of faith and the promotion of justice." In that mission, a serious effort must be made to understand the socio-economic and political situation within which evangelization occurs. Hence:

> We cannot be excused from making the most rigorous possible political and social analysis of our situation. This will require the utilization of the various sciences, sacred and profane, and of the various disciplines, speculative and practical, and all of this demands intense and specialized studies. Nothing should excuse us, either, from undertaking a searching discernment into our situation from the pastoral and apostolic point of view. From analysis and discernment will come committed action; from the experience of action will come insight into how to proceed further [No. 44].

The call to analysis is further specified in this document with the help of several questions:

> The process of evaluation and discernment must be brought to bear principally on the following: the identification and analysis of the problems involved in the service of faith and the promotion of justice and the review and renewal of our apostolic commitments. Where do we live? Where do we work? How? With whom? What really is our involvement with, dependence on, or commitment to ideologies and power centers? [No. 74]

In the fall of 1977, representatives of the leadership of women's and men's religious congregations in the United States, Latin America, and Canada, met in Montreal. This Third Inter-American Conference of Religious issued a strong call—especially influenced by the Latin Americans—to commit religious to pastoral planning that incorporated both social analysis and theological reflection. The call was repeated in Cleveland in August 1978, at "CONVERGENCE '78"—the historic joint meeting of the Leadership Conference of Women Religious and the Conference of Major Superiors of Men. In their final statement, the religious superiors pledged:

> Realizing that we lack full understanding of our social, economic, and political life, we commit ourselves to structural analysis and theological reflection.

Since the Cleveland CONVERGENCE meeting, there have been numerous lectures, workshops, and seminars across the country to introduce leadership—lay, religious, and clerical—to the topic of social analysis in relation to pastoral planning.

Some people may fear that "social analysis" is simply another fad, the "in-thing" to do. However, it makes sense that church leadership should move toward a greater emphasis on social analysis in making pastoral decisions. Social analysis is simply an extension of the principle of discernment, moving from the personal realm to the social realm. Just as the insights of psychology (psycho-analysis) have been incorporated into the process of personal discernment, the insights of the social sciences (social analysis) will assist the church in the process of corporate discernment, and ultimately, in the fulfillment of its apostolic mission.

Analysis and Theology

Let us recall once again the pastoral circle discussed at the beginning of this chapter. Social analysis is but *one* moment in that circle. While it is an indispensable step toward effective action on behalf of justice, it must be complemented by theological reflection and pastoral planning. None of these parts can be totally isolated; theology is not restricted to that moment explicitly called "theological reflection." In a wider sense, all the moments of the circle are part of an expanded definition of theology. All are linked and overlap.

Among various schools of social analysis today, there is much controversy concerning the fundamental assumptions of human sciences, their relation to human values, the nature and division of the distinct disciplines, etc. These controversies are the result of differing visions of the meaning, structure, and process of humanity's common life, struggle, and destiny. Thus, we can say that social analysis contains within itself, implicitly or explicitly, a theology of life. The theological process has already begun in what appears to be a secular analysis of society.

In this study, we will concentrate on social analysis, the second moment of the pastoral circle. Yet, we do so in a theological context—that is, one inspired by a faith commitment. For the present, however, we postpone more extended reflections on the third and fourth moments of the circle, namely, theological reflection and pastoral planning.

WHAT IS ANALYSIS?

Social analysis can be defined as the effort to obtain a more complete picture of a social situation by exploring its *historical and structural relationships*. Social analysis serves as a tool that permits us to grasp the reality with which we are dealing—*"la realidad"* so often referred to in Latin America.

Social analysis explores reality in a variety of dimensions. Sometimes it focuses on isolated *issues*, such as unemployment, inflation, or hunger. At other times, it focuses on the *policies* that address these issues, such as job training, monetary control, or food aid programs. Using social analysis, one might further investigate the broad *structures* of our economic, political, social, and cultural institutions, from whence such issues arise and to which policies are addressed.

Reaching beyond issues, policies, and structures, social analysis ultimately focuses on *systems*. There are many dimensions to these systems as well. We can speak of a social system's *economic* design as a distinct functional region or subsystem. We can analyze the *political* order of a system and its *cultural* foundation. Finally, we can analyze the social system in terms of *levels*—primary groups, local communities, nation-states, and even in terms of the world system.

The social system needs to be analyzed both in terms of time—*historical* analysis—and space—*structural* analysis. Historical analysis is a study of the changes of a social system through time. Structural analysis provides a cross section of a system's framework in a given moment of time. A sense of both the historical and structural dimensions is necessary for a comprehensive analysis.

Finally, we can distinguish the *objective* and *subjective* dimensions of reality in our analysis. The objective dimension includes the various organizations, behavior patterns, and institutions that take on external structural expressions. The subjective dimension includes consciousness, values, and ideologies. These elements must be analyzed in order to understand the assumptions operative in any given social situation. The questions posed by social analysis unmask the underlying values that shape the perspectives and decisions of those acting within a given situation.

Although social analysis is used to "break down" social reality, that reality is considerably more complex than any picture painted by the analytic process. No social system ever fits a pure or ideal model. Capitalism, for example, exists in many forms, influenced by various cultural, geographic, and national experiences. The goal is not to fit reality into our preconceived analytical boxes, but to let our analysis be shaped by the richness of the reality.

The Limits of Social Analysis

As we begin to use social analysis as a pastoral tool, we need to be aware of its limits. While our cautions are rather obvious, it is helpful to articulate them. (We will return to this theme, the limits of analysis, at the end of the study.)

First, social analysis is not designed to provide an immediate answer to the question, what do we do? That is the task of strategy or planning. Social analysis unfolds the context within which a program for social change can be outlined, but does not provide a blueprint for action.

Social analysis is to social strategy what diagnosis is to treatment. Both analysis and diagnosis are necessary prerequisites to the cure of social and physical ills. However, they cannot themselves provide that cure. After diagnosing a particular health problem, a doctor is able to describe the problem in a clear and complete fashion. However, treatment or therapy is another task. Similarly, very detailed analysis of a particular social situation will not provide programmatic answers. Social analysis offers broad parameters within which specific tactics and strategies can be suggested, but it does not formulate them.

This caution is important. As interest in social analysis increases among lay, religious, professional, and community organizations, there is a danger that the contributions of social analysis will be exaggerated. Regarding social analysis as a complex panacea, people may assume that the task can be accomplished only by "outside experts"—individuals who are professionally skilled in the tools of social analysis. They might look to these professionals to provide all the answers. However, "experts" are useful only in so far as they expose the wider context of the situation and train local people in the use of analytical tools. Ultimately, it is the local people who must offer specific approaches to social problems and concrete steps toward their resolution. These people are the only ones who have experienced the particular situation; their expertise in designing solutions should always be respected.

Second, social analysis is not an esoteric activity for intellectuals. All of us use the tool every day in a variety of ways. We use it implicitly whenever we relate one specific event or issue to another, whenever we choose one course of action over another. The framework that makes those relationships and choices possible contains an implicit social analysis. More detailed social analysis makes that implicit analysis explicit and more precise.

Third, social analysis is not value-free. This point is extremely important. Social analysis is not a neutral approach, a purely "scientific" and "objective" view of reality. Of course, we should try to be clear, precise, reasoned, and logical. However, in our very choice of topics, in our manner of approach, in our questions, in our openness to the results of our analysis, we reveal our values and our biases. We never enter into an analysis without some prior commitment—implicit or explicit. That commitment colors our work and the work of others engaged in similar processes. For example, a person serving a community organization in a poor neighborhood in East St. Louis will move into social analysis with a different commitment from a person surveying the retail market future for a large department store in downtown St. Louis.

We will return later to the value dimension of social analysis. It is mentioned at the outset only to emphasize that social analysis in the service of pastoral planning requires a distinctive set of values. In the very process of analysis itself, we need to wrestle with the biases of our consciousness, critiquing our deepest assumptions, exploring the new horizons that are opened for us.

Difficulties

If social analysis is so important, why is it so often ignored by people engaged in pastoral planning and action? Or, if not ignored, why does it seem to be so difficult? The answers can be found, in part, in the complexity of our society and its tendency toward change and controversy.

First, society in the United States is growing more and more complex. We have moved a long way from the simple and plain living of our ancestors. Our social system is now a bewildering maze of people, institutions, networks, bureaucracies, and machines. This complexity makes us feel almost powerless—even fatalistic. To attempt to analyze this complexity could make us feel even more confused. We fear that the more we study, the more bewildered we will become. Eventually, we will be unable to act at all. Dr. Martin Luther King, Jr. referred to this predicament as the "paralysis of analysis."

Second, social analysis is difficult because our society is constantly changing. Yesterday's analysis may not be valid today. Tomorrow's changes may undercut today's assumptions. The particular analysis we choose to help us interpret the new situation will, in turn, shape the remedy we ultimately find. It will determine whether we embark upon a creative, ineffective, or destructive social response. Given our continual state of change, we must constantly adapt our analysis to new situations, remaining open to critical evaluation. Above all, we must avoid dogmatism and the rigidity of fixed ideas.

Third, to enter into social analysis is to enter the realm of the controversial. The existence of controversy will make our task even more difficult. As noted earlier, social analysis is not value-free. We always choose an analysis that is implicitly linked to some ideological tradition. The claim to have no ideology is itself an ideological position! Locating ourselves within some vision of society—whether it be one of the many interpretations of capitalism, socialism, feudalism, tribalism, etc.—we interact with various social and political movements, many of them fiercely antagonistic to each other.

The reluctance to move toward social analysis can be explained, in part, by this element of controversy. Behind our protests that social analysis is too difficult or irrelevant may be a fear that it is really too "radical." If we were to examine the institutions and processes of our society and of our church, would we not become continual questioners and doubters—driven to "radical" responses?

For these three reasons, then, analysis is a difficult task: it is complex, never ending, and always controversial. Given these obstacles, we might ask ourselves, why bother? Why is it really important? Because of our heritage of pragmatism, these reactions are instinctive for many people in the United States. Oriented toward "practicality" and the immediate attainment of goals, our culture is not conducive to analytical endeavors. Faced with complexities, we want to charge ahead, implementing immediate, albeit *ad hoc*, solutions. The Anglo-American bias rejects the theoretical and the ideal in favor of the practical "workable" solution. We have a tendency to believe that theorizing is a luxury and that laborious analytical explorations are simply a waste of time. "Mission Impossible" was not only a popular television show; it is a mindset that we bring to bear on social challenges. To be asked to step back and look at the larger picture is a cultural challenge to the American tradition.

Our traditional U.S. heritage as a nation of problem solvers has generally served us well. The pragmatic gift has made rich contributions to our history. But, we are entering a fundamentally new era in U.S. history. In this era, pragmatic genius needs to be supplemented by a more thorough-going social analysis.

Opportunities and Limits

We are entering a difficult era. Prior to the 1970s, the United States was a land of continually expanding social opportunities. Today, however, the United States is becoming a land of decreasing opportunities. The predominant cultural theme underlying the expansionist era of our history was the "frontier." The new theme pressing on our consciousness today is the "limit" to our wealth and growth.

While the analysis of this new era varies, that a new era exists is widely accepted as fact. New political groups have emerged to face the challenge. First, people who claim to be in the political *Center* have stressed the necessity for a "new realism," suggesting that we are leaving an age of bounty and entering into one of austerity. This theme, developed by the so-called "neo-conservative" movement, has influenced some writers to attack what they call the "moralisms" of social liberals who, they claim, do not understand the new structural constraints of our social system. These voices are frank about the limits of the new situation—the need to conserve energy, to get along with less, to lower our expectations—but they are less harsh in their solutions than a second political group, the New Right.

The *New Right* is strategizing to become the leading social force in the new era. It realizes that the solutions of the political Center can no longer meet the challenges of society. "Austerity" is not an appealing theme for people who are losing their jobs! Consequently, the New Right has mounted an attack against "big government," advocating the restoration of a *"laissez-faire"* (unregulated) economy reminiscent of nineteenth-century capitalism. The responses of the New Right, if implemented, would bring about widespread suffering among the voiceless and powerless worldwide. Yet, this group has gained ground in the United States political arena, mainly because ordinary people don't know where to turn.

A third group is beginning to form on the political *Left*. This group suggests that the emerging limits to U.S. society will aggravate social conflict within the nation. The new Left claims that the restructuring of capitalism is compelling much of society to shoulder an unjust burden. This group argues that we must search for a new form of society, one that is not dominated by giant multinational corporations, international financial institutions, or repressive governments.

The setting of limits need not result in the end of opportunity. But the limitations *do* mean that our past assumptions of endless expansion within open and growing frontiers are no longer valid. New opportunities can be discovered, but only within the new limits. In order to discover these opportunities, however, we must deepen our social analysis, stimulate our creative imagination, and broaden our vision. The "new frontier" of today is imagination and social creativity, within the bounds of limits that have been imposed upon us. Because the old consensus is breaking down throughout society, this task will be extremely important, but also very difficult. The arduousness of the task raises a special challenge for social analysis and constitutes one of the main reasons for its importance at this time. How can we discover a broad and challenging vision that will give new life to the social struggle?

Fragmentation or Solidarity

Without a new vision, social in-fighting over scarce resources (jobs, fuel, food, etc.) will increase. The response to in-fighting can take two forms—further fragmentation or solidarity.

If *fragmentation* predominates, it will mean that the social system will be analyzed in terms of its parts, rather than the whole. It will mean immediate, short-range, piecemeal gains by some, at the expense of permanent, long-range, holistic gains by all. Each group will be concerned only about itself, no matter what the consequences for other groups. Such fragmentation could aggravate our social disintegration and yield a negative-sum game.

Unfortunately our heritage of social pragmatism—one that is not linked to a deeper social analysis—leaves us ill-equipped for the long-range, holistic perspective. If we focus only on the pieces—our piece of the pie or anyone else's—and fail to see the larger picture, we will not be able to work together for a strategy that benefits all. We will be easily confused, readily manipulated. Thus, if short-range pragmatism predominates, the tensions among racial and ethnic groupings will grow. Stress in families, between sexes, and among competing interest groups within the nation and in the international arena will increase. Groups that are being hurt by the new stage of the system could find themselves pitted against each other to the ultimate detriment of all.

If *solidarity* is to predominate, a deeper level of analysis needs to emerge. But such analysis will evolve only if we press beyond the pragmatic approach of the past—without abandoning its innovative qualities. Pragmatism can be sustained, but only within a broader framework of structural and systemic analysis of our common social struggle and the linkages of all issues and causes. To achieve that solidarity in action on behalf of justice is a great challenge to all of us using social analysis as a pastoral tool.

ELEMENTS OF ANALYSIS

In any analysis of our social reality, we explore a number of society's elements. Among them are: (1) the *historical* dimensions of a situation; (2) its *structural* elements; (3) the various *divisions* of society; and (4) the multiple *levels* of the issues involved.

History

Central to any social analysis is the historical question, where are we coming from and where are we going? Taking history seriously is a liberating exercise, since it places current events and challenges into a perspective. History relativizes the immediate and situates us in a larger context by clarifying our past and offering insights into our future. The non-historical approach is basically *status quo*-oriented, since it lifts the present out of context and treats it as an absolute existing in a vacuum.

Some approaches to social analysis can be non-historical. For example, a strictly "comparative" methodology tends to abstract the present from history. One economic system is compared with another—e.g., capitalism vs. socialism—without stressing the point that these systems have reality only in continually evolving, concrete historical situations. They are not immutable abstractions—what sociologists call "ideal types"—but realities immersed in the day-to-day evolution of life. Failure to attend to the historical dimension can make comparisons, at best, inadequate, and at worst, misleading.

When history is taken seriously, we develop a historical consciousness. This historical consciousness regards the passage of time not simply in terms of natural processes such as the seasons of the year or the biological cycles of growth and decay. Rather, time, in this case, marks a series of specific events in which we are consciously involved and which we can consciously influence. Attending to this consciousness frees people from the tyranny of history's "invisible forces" which, in actuality, are little more than the power of other people to determine the course of our lives. Paulo Freire, the great Brazilian educator, speaks of the dire need for this kind of critical consciousness, because it liberates people from the role of historical *objects*, empowering them to become its *subjects*—i.e., agents of change.

We can distinguish two moments in any kind of historical awareness: (1) a *scientific moment* that carefully analyzes the past, and (2) an *intuitive moment* that probes the future.

The *scientific moment* of historical awareness describes social change according to various stages, identifying the evolution of key structures, actors, concepts, etc., over a given period of time. In Chapter 4, such a historical description is presented in a discussion of the stages of industrial capitalism. However, let us indicate at this point a few examples of the scientific moment of historical awareness.

Take, for example, the immigration of people from Europe to the United States at the end of the nineteenth and the beginning of the twentieth centuries. We can see three different stages of immigration—as experienced by the Irish, Italian, Eastern European, and other people who flocked to the U.S. shores.

First, there was a stage of *separation*, when the new immigrants segregated themselves from the frequently hostile environment in the new land. Native languages, foods, and customs were honored and strengthened. Second, there was a stage of *assimilation*, a period in which the first and second generations born in this country sometimes forgot (or never learned) the old languages and often shunned the traditional neighborhoods, foods, and customs. Some of the daughters and sons of immigrants came into the "mainstream" of U.S. social, economic, and political life. We are currently experiencing a third stage of immigration, that of *identification*. Identification does not mean a return to separation or isolation; rather, it signifies a new pride in ethnic roots, a new sense of one's special culture, and a rejection of the homogenization of society.

Another example of the scientific moment of historical awareness can be found in the shifting forms of racism in the United States. The first form of racism concerning blacks in this country occurred in the plantation economy—outside the emerging industrial economy. The kindest name for this type of racism is *paternalism*. The main racial conflict occurred between the white planter class and the black slave population.

With emancipation, black citizens in the United States faced a new form of racism. They were thrown into an industrial economy where white labor competed with black labor, and both were at the mercy of the white entrepreneurial class. The result was a two-tiered or dual labor market—with blacks most frequently at the bottom of the ladder, holding the lowest paying and most menial jobs. This second stage of racism is called *discrimination*.

We are now facing yet another stage of racism. With a shrinking industrial economy, "structural unemployment" is heavily concentrated among non-whites. An urban "permanent underclass" is developing—a class of people who are isolated from the economic mainstream and ignored. This third stage of racism is called *marginalization*.

A second moment in historical consciousness—less rational and precise than the scientific moment—is the *intuitive moment*. Questioning history from this perspective, we might ask, where are we heading today? What will the world be like five or ten years hence if things continue as they are going today? What directions will the United States take in the future, and what will be the consequences for the Third World?

Historical awareness through the intuitive moment is extremely popular today, stimulating the discussion of various historical "scenarios," "projections," and "alternative futures." Its popularity appears to be one consequence of the rapid pace of change we are all experiencing. We look to the future in order to avoid "future shock." However, it is important to remember that our projections into the future tell us something about our understanding of the present and our appreciation of the past. For example, a vision of an improved future implies both judgments on the past and present, as well as the perception of opportunities for progress in the future.

A Christian is careful to note that the Spirit of Jesus is active in history, operating in the concrete events of persons and communities. Hence, a historical consciousness for the Christian also means a commitment to reading the "signs of the times," the indications of Jesus' Spirit acting in history, calling us forward, challenging our present positions. In *Pacem in Terris* (1963), Pope John XXIII reminded us that the great historical movements of our day—specifically the rise of new nations, the struggle of workers, and the emerging role of women—can be read as "signs of the times" with special messages for all.

Structures

Social analysis looks sharply at the structures of our society, at the institutions within which we live our social lives. These social structures—government, law, education, business, labor, church, family, etc.—are realities that need to be understood if our action for justice is to be effective.

Social justice is itself a structural question, not simply a personal matter. For example, I may not personally be a racist, or a male chauvinist. I may treat women and people of other races as equals, in speech, attitudes, and behavior. However, this personal action does not address the deep justice issues of racism or sexism—unemployment, lack of educational opportunities, discriminatory pay, or lack of access to decision-making positions. These are structural questions.

With the aid of social analysis, we can identify the key operative structures in a given situation and move beyond personal considerations toward specific structural changes. Without such an analysis, we may become paralyzed by those questions so often asked in discussions of social justice: "But how can such-and-such a corporation be engaged in unjust practices when Mr. So-and-So is an outstanding Christian and personal benefactor of many good causes?" At issue is not the goodness of the individual person living within a given system. Rather, it is the system itself that is called into question.

The problem of migrant labor is a good illustration of this point. The issue is not whether an individual grower in the Fresno Valley of California is a good or a malevolent person. Rather, the issue is the system of economic relationships between owner and producer and factors such as labor availability, land tenure, access to market, competition, etc., that lead to the exploitation of the unprotected migrant worker.

Similarly, the problems of Appalachian farmers, whose land is being strip-mined, or those of elderly inner-city residents whose apartments are being converted into condominiums, are basically rooted, not in the personal character of mine-operators or landlords, but in the economic system that encourages the kind of energy industry and real estate business that exists in the United States. Social analysis moves us from persons to structures.

We will look first at the *economic structures* of society—the business and commercial institutions, the industrial and agricultural sectors. The economic structures shape the basic patterns of production, distribution, exchange, and consumption within a society. Today we tend to think of economic structures in terms of contrasts—between capitalism and socialism, between "free enterprise" and planned economies, etc. However, these terms have many different meanings. Through analysis we may ask questions about the kind of production (e.g., highly technological—i.e., capital-intensive—or employment generating—i.e., labor-intensive), the paths of distribution (e.g., monopolistic or widely shared), the conditions of exchange (e.g., interest rates for loans), and the patterns of consumption (e.g., conducive to waste or to conservation of scarce resources).

The pursuit of such questions gives us insight into the nature of the classes controlling the economy and the values that determine its operations. The myth that the economy is guided by an "invisible hand" is just that—a myth! (For in-depth economic analyses that expose the myth of "neutral" corporations operating in a "free market" system, see Richard J. Barnet and Ronald E. Müller, *Global Reach: The Power of the Multinational Corporations,* New York: Simon and Schuster, 1974; and Charles Lindbloom, *Politics and Markets: The World's Political-Economic Systems,* New York: Basic Books, Inc., 1977. The immensely popular book by E. F. Schumacher, *Small is Beautiful: Economics as if People Mattered,* New York: Harper & Row, 1973, has demolished the assumption that economics is a value-free science, a technical/mechanical approach to management.)

Second, we look at the *political structures* of society, the institutional concentrations of power within a community. These may be the formal structures of representative government at the federal, state, and local levels. Or, the structures may be less formal—influential groupings of individuals, networks of organizations, interest group lobbies, social classes, trade unions, churches, and coalitions for *ad hoc* purposes. Social analysis of political structures allows us to determine where and by whom key decisions are made, how much popular participation is involved, and the prospects for the enactment of those decisions.

Finally, we look at the *cultural structures* that serve as the institutional bases for the dreams, myths, and symbols of society. It might seem strange to speak of "institutionalizing" dreams, but, in our highly organized modern society, we do this in a variety of ways. The culture of the United States, for example, is a marvelous mixture of numerous ethnic heritages—those of Native Americans, African slaves, and peasants from Europe, Asia, and Latin America. What are the dominant cultural strains in a society, and what happens to the less-dominant strains? Such efforts as cultural preservation and recovery (e.g., through bilingual schools, etc.) have important consequences for U.S. society. What social-psychological aspects influence the course of events (e.g., national feelings of malaise, or stirred feelings of patriotism, etc.)?

In a social analysis that seriously considers all these structures, *institutional alliances* between various structures must also be examined. For instance, what are the connections between the economic structures operative in a region of the country and the political structures that have evolved? What is the relationship between the economic power of multinational corporations and the political power dominant in some developing countries (i.e., military dictatorships)?

The communications media offers striking examples of such institutional alliances. A newspaper can be extremely influential in the economic, political, and cultural aspects of community life—through its advertising policy, its endorsement of political candidates, and its reporting of the arts. When the owners of that newspaper also control other papers, weekly magazines, and television stations, a tremendous concentration of power occurs. Recall the institutional intricacies portrayed in the film *Network*, which described the cut-throat world of national television and the social and political consequences of those entanglements.

Societal Divisions

Although it may be belaboring the obvious, we want to point out that social analysis enables us to see more clearly the divisions of society according to *race, sex, age, class, ethnicity, religion, geography,* etc. These divisions exist, whether we like it or not. Sometimes they are more immediately apparent and more directly operative than at other times. However, they are always present and as such, should be key elements in any social analysis. To ignore them is to bypass the total picture of reality.

It is important to recognize these divisions for two reasons. First, the consequences of a particular event in a given social situation—e.g., an economic upheaval such as a recession—do not affect all people in the same way. Second, some divisions in a pluralistic society such as the United States, if played against each other, can be a disruptive force in the process of social change. Consider, for example, the competition between blacks and other poor ethnic minorities for jobs in a shrinking labor market. As long as other minorities are viewed as the cause rather than the victims of the problem, the systemic cause will not be addressed. However, if these same divisions are viewed analytically within a larger social picture, we can take advantage of opportunities for solidarity in the promotion of a common good. An example of such solidarity can be found in the coalitions of consumer and labor groups that focus on energy issues.

We sometimes speak as if all people enjoy—or suffer—social reality in the same fashion. While we know that this is not true, our speech patterns occasionally say something else. For instance, the most commonly reported figure for unemployment—the one to which certain emergency federal legislation is pegged—lumps all the represented groups together. Yet we know—through experience and as a result of other official statistics that provide a further breakdown of the figures—that unemployment is more highly concentrated among non-whites and youth. Again, we know that anti-union attitudes and anti-union legislation such as "right-to-work" laws generally mean lower wages. But we may fail to note that these laws and attitudes are particularly hard on young black female workers in the South. Or, we may speak of the "establishment" or the "influentials" in politics and business, without averting to the fact that they are predominantly white, Anglo-Saxon, Protestant males, heavily concentrated in the northeastern section of our country.

Social analysis should make us aware of these divisions, so the intricate dimensions of reality will not be ignored as we shape our responses. To ignore these divisions in the pluralistic U.S. society is to play into the hands of those who would manipulate whites against non-whites, men against women, old against young, and region against region. Such manipulation preserves a status quo in which a few are dominant over the many.

Are there really "classes" in the traditional sense, here in the United States? A discussion about social divisions must inevitably raise this question. The class issue in modern society is extremely complex. It is especially complicated in the United States because of our history of immigration, mobility, and rapid industrialization. Certainly, we can say that socio-economic status—a combination of income, property, education, employment, etc.—does exist as a determinant to social relationships in this country. A deeper "class analysis," however, enables us to see who makes the major economic and political decisions that affect large segments of the population. A "class analysis" can be made by asking three simple questions:

1. Who makes the decisions?
2. Who benefits from the decisions?
3. Who bears the cost of the decisions?

Consider, for example, a decision to "renew" a particular section of a city. Frequently, such a decision has been made by local government officials—perhaps an elected city council—who do not represent the people living in the area, in conjunction with real estate, construction, and banking interests. Middle and upper-income couples will benefit from the expansion of commercial zones. Lower-income people, frequently non-white and/or elderly, will be displaced to another section of the city, usually without comparable advantages, and almost certainly without improvements. Similarly, at the national level, major economic decisions for the country (e.g., interest rates, money supply, etc.) are made by less than one percent of the population.

Levels of Issues

Finally, it should be noted that issues occur at various levels— the local, regional, national, and international levels. The framework chosen by the social analyst will indicate the level of the issue; even more important, it will indicate the relationships between levels.

For example, an issue such as the impact of "redlining" on the renewal of a neighborhood has a predominantly local focus. (When a bank refuses to make loans to a particular geographic section of a city because of its "high economic risk"—i.e., its high concentration of racial or ethnic minorities—it draws a "red line" around that particular area on the map.) Or, the issue may have a fundamentally international focus—e.g., the "balance of trade" between the United States and Japan. (The balance of trade indicates whether we are importing more than we are exporting and vice versa.)

Responses to issues will vary according to their particular "levels." However, there are strong interconnections between levels; these relationships need to be recognized if effective responses are to be made. Let us again look at the example of "redlining." A predominantly local issue, redlining may be related to a significant regional issue, e.g., the decision of the banking industry to "disinvest" from the decaying northern industrial cities—in favor of making loans to suburban areas or to the growing industrial areas of the South. The "snowbelt/sunbelt" tension—largely the result of the northern industries moving to southern regions of the United States where labor is unorganized and cheaper—impacts directly on neighborhoods in the northern cities. Similarly, energy decisions that may affect whole regions—e.g., the consequences of strip-mining in Appalachia—are tied to international issues such as the price of oil and the relationship of the United States to OPEC nations.

The analysis of issues according to their various levels and interconnections is important because it rectifies the misconception that local issues are in competition with global issues. One of the most significant developments in the U.S. social justice movement in recent years has been the recognition that the dichotomy between domestic and international problems is an inaccurate representation of reality. All of the problems are part of a whole. The relation of the parts to the whole can be understood with the help of a few fundamental questions: Who has power? For whom is it used? Guided by what values? With what vision of the future?

These questions are appropriate—and revealing—at every issue level.

SUMMARY/CONCLUSION

By devoting this chapter to the introduction of social analysis as a tool of pastoral practice, we have opted for an approach that could have confusing consequences. We have chosen to *talk* about social analysis rather than *do* social analysis. Nonetheless, we believe that it is important to describe at the outset what social analysis attempts to do, why it is difficult, and what aspects of reality it explores. The approach we have described locates the task of social analysis within a "pastoral circle" aimed at action on behalf of justice.

In the following chapters we will apply our analysis to a variety of the social challenges facing us today. In the light of what we have said in this introductory chapter, it should be clear that our approach will be:

- *historical*, **i.e., discerning the distinct structural contexts of distinct periods and the different tasks of strategy in each period.**
- *structural*, **i.e., emphasizing the importance of understanding how society is generated and structured and how social institutions interrelate in social space.**
- *value-laden*, **i.e., oriented toward social justice, particularly for the poor.**
- *non-dogmatic*, **i.e., drawing upon a variety of perspectives and "schools" of analysis.**
- *action oriented*, **i.e., promoting responses by individuals and groups to the pressing social problems of today.**

Chapter 2

Social Analysis
and Social Change

As noted in the preceding chapter, key to our work for social justice is an understanding of social change. By clarifying the different processes of change, social analysis helps us to see the dynamics of the social reality and enables us to respond effectively. There are, of course, many interpretations of change. In this chapter, we offer three interpretative models of the dynamics of change within society: a *traditional* model, a *liberal* model, and a *radical* model.

As we explore the dynamics of change, we are really probing for fundamental interpretations of the social forces operative in society. Our recognition that the world is not static, but that reality is basically a *process*, is a significant first step. To paraphrase a well-known expression of Cardinal Newman, "To live is to change, and to live long is to change much."

Change can imply *conflict*; the social forces that move in history sometimes oppose each other. The three interpretative models of change (traditional, liberal, and radical) also represent different perspectives of the significance of social conflict.

It is important to note that the models of change discussed in this chapter are historically-rooted interpretations. They are not simply abstract models, whose theoretical merits can be weighed in isolation from the concrete events of history. While they represent competing schools of thought at the present time, they also represent a historic succession of perspectives on society and the

31

ordering of social relationships. The nature of this succession will become more obvious as we explore the details of each particular model.

Within our discussion of each model, we will show how its particular type of social analysis identifies: (1) the interpretation of time and space; (2) the governing principle of society; (3) the underlying social metaphor; and, (4) the attitude toward conflict (for further elaboration, see Chart A).

CHART A: INTERPRETATIVE MODELS OF CHANGE

	Traditional	Liberal	Radical
View of Time:	Cyclical	Evolutionary	Transformative
View of Space:	Organic	Pluralistic	Interdependent
Governing Principle:	Authoritarian (Order)	Managerial (Balance)	Participative (Community)
Underlying Metaphor:	Biological (Human Body)	Mechanistic (Machine)	Artistic (Work of Art)
View of Conflict	Deviant	Superficial	Creative

THE TRADITIONAL MODEL

Historically, the traditional model for interpreting social change or the dynamics of society has been the dominant one. Simply expressed, the traditional view is that nothing changes fundamentally; society's structures remain much the same as they always have been. This model is a *cyclical/organic/authoritarian* model. The basic interpretative metaphor it employs is *biological*—viewing society as an organism analogous to the human body. Let us examine each of these elements of the traditional model.

According to this model, social time follows a "biological" pattern; hence, it is *cyclical*. There is change in the world, but the change constantly repeats the same pattern—birth, maturity, death—moving along a cyclical path. Change is the rhythm of nature itself, expressed in the cycle of the seasons of the year and in the human life cycle. The separate parts of past, present, and future are integrated into the single historical whole of the cycle.

Similarly, social space is conceived in biological terms; it is perceived to be *organic*. The traditional model finds no unrelated parts in society—no atomistic, individual persons, no autonomous social classes or groups with conflicting self-interests, no sharp separation between functional regions like church and state. There is only a single organic social fabric, organized around the "common good," to which all the parts are subordinated.

The governing principle operative in this model is *authoritarian* or hierarchical. Society is considered to be an ascending social pyramid, controlled at the top with little participation from the bottom. The few direct the many. Those who are in control are the arbiters of the social process: how the society should function, how order should be kept, how the "common good" should be defined and served, and what represents deviant or pathological threats—internally or externally—to the life of society.

The basic interpretative metaphor employed by this model is that of the *human body*. Throughout time, the body is born, grows, decays, and is regenerated. In space, its various parts are integrally related; all its internal functions and external operations are controlled by the head.

What does this model contribute to an understanding of the dynamics of change within society? How does it guide responses to challenges to the status quo?

According to the traditional model, significant historical change is viewed as deviant or pathological; thus, the best response to a challenge to the order of things is either: (1) to smooth over the challenge and absorb it into the present system; or, (2) to reject it outright. Take, for example, a foreign object that is introduced into a human body—e.g., a transplanted kidney. Either the body accepts the new organ completely, or the organ is rejected, and the body tries to "expel" it. Likewise, according to this model of social change, the particular challenge is either absorbed into the system, or it is rejected—that is, suppressed.

Historically, we can see how the traditional model of change guided the classical societies of Europe and influenced the development of the Western Catholic church. A landed aristocracy, hierarchically structured through nobility and high clergy, constituted the ruling elite. At best, this form of leadership served as a paternalistic guardian of the "common good," exercising a *noblesse oblige* toward the lower classes. At worst, it collapsed into despotic absolutism. In either case, its reaction to a challenge to the status quo was the same—absorption or suppression. Such rule was justified on ideological grounds by appeals to the "divine right of kings," the demands of "social order," the preservation of "tradition" and "sound doctrine," and the assertion that "this is the way things have always been done."

In the United States, such a defense of the *status quo* is clearly illustrated in the conservative response to racial conflict and the challenge to contemporary patterns of black-white relationships. As the conflict deepened in the 1960s and '70s, "traditionalists" defended "law and order," cultivated "Uncle Tom" leadership among the black population, and rejected all demands for a shift in race relations. We witnessed the enactment of these responses during the early days of the civil rights movement, as whites sought to maintain the "traditional" order of society—an order that left blacks in a socially, economically, and politically inferior position. We heard people say that it was not "healthy" to have so much social turmoil and to attempt to change patterns so integral to the U.S. experience. *Order* and *harmony* are the basic social virtues according to the traditional model.

THE LIBERAL MODEL

The liberal model of change has, to a large extent, replaced the traditional model in contemporary society. Concepts such as "pragmatism" and "pluralism" are extremely important in this model. Unlike the model that preceded it, the liberal model does not oppose change, harkening back to a golden era of the past. Rather, this model is future-oriented and at home with change. Simply expressed, the liberal model holds that society is in flux and a continuous flow of events impacts upon the social order in a significant fashion. However, these events do not fundamentally change its structure.

The liberal model is *evolutionary/pluralistic/managerial*. Its basic interpretative metaphor is *mechanistic*. It draws on Newtonian physics, just as the traditional model drew on classical biology. Following the same patterns used in our review of the traditional model, we can examine the meaning of the liberal model.

According to this model, social time is linear or *evolutionary*. The movement in history is not cyclical, but progressive; important new events are always unfolding. The best approach to change is to embrace it, stepping forward into the future, rather than retreating into the past. Change is viewed as "progress." It proceeds along a continuum in which society gradually moves onward and upward. The movement of society follows this continuum; it is not outside of, beyond, or over and against certain fixed boundaries. The past, according to this model, is often viewed as the enemy of the future, a time when change was held at bay and progress obstructed.

Social space, according to the liberal model, is *pluralistic*. Its structure is not seen as a collective whole, but as a cluster of free or isolated parts—atomistic individuals, conflicting interest groups with no organic linkages, disparate nations, etc. Functional regions are distinct and unrelated (e.g., economics, politics, and culture). It is assumed in this model that the "common good" is not the direct object of social concern, but results indirectly from the self-actualization of all the parts. In economic terms, an "invisible hand" guides competition in the "free market" system for the benefit of all. In political terms, the parts are actuated as interest groups; in cultural terms they express themselves through "free thought." In this view, a healthy society is marked by individualism and innovation; it thrives in an expanding, competitive situation.

The governing principle operative in the liberal model is *managerial*. The interaction of the separate parts within the system requires rational management. This management needs to accomplish two basic tasks. First, it must keep the parts from moving to one of two extremes—anarchy, in which social cohesiveness is shattered, or authoritarianism, in which social, economic, and political power are over-centralized, i.e., concentrated in the hands of a few. Second, the task of management is to keep the concert of parts moving along the expanding trajectory of progress.

The liberal managerial style does not, as mentioned earlier, directly and positively promote the "common good." Rather, it "encourages" it negatively, by strengthening "countervailing forces" and offering "opportunities" for progress. "Balancing" the system is extremely important. *Balance* is the key social virtue in this model.

The emphasis on balance is evident in the basic interpretative metaphor employed by the liberal model—the *machine*. An intricate collection of individual parts, the machine is not organically integrated—that is, its parts are not related through some intrinsic order. Rather, it is mechanically held together—that is, its parts are related externally through counter-balancing tensions.

The liberal model responds to challenges to the status quo in ways significantly different from those suggested by the traditional model. If society is perceived to be continually changing, the best response to some specific challenge is to determine how to manage it. The competing interests must be played off against one another. A school of "conflict management" has even been formed—one that has had significant influence on contemporary international affairs.

Historically, the liberal model of social change has been influential since the breakdown of traditional societies. The ideal of a well-balanced society in nineteenth- and twentieth-century Europe and North America was a "market" environment within which unrelated individual parts interacted competitively through "free enterprise" (economics), liberal democracy (politics), and "free thought" (culture).

The role of liberal government was first defined as "*laissez-faire*"—that is, it was required to leave social and economic forces alone. Its task was conceived negatively—to prevent one part from dominating another part and thereby to assure a "free" operation of the market. The classic political expression of the liberal model can be found in Number 10 of *The Federalist Papers*, written by James Madison. Madison argued that the competing interests in a pluralistic society would keep the United States free, the government modest, and the people prospering. The classic economic expression is the economic model of Adam Smith. The classic cultural expression is liberalism.

During a later period, liberalism evolved into a more social form, which is what we mean by the term "liberal" in contemporary American politics. By contrast, we use the word "conservative" in contemporary American politics to refer to the philosophy and policies of early liberalism. The two forms of liberalism saw the role of government in fundamentally different ways. According to social liberalism, society is composed of large blocs (business, labor, government), that need to be managed by a social welfare state. According to early liberalism—or contemporary American "conservatism"—the competing forces of society should be left alone and allowed to play out their normal course in a *laissez-faire* state. (The difficulty with the dual definition of liberalism is compounded by the fact that in Europe, "liberal" refers to the early use of the term, while the term "conservative" refers to a traditionalist perspective.)

Again, we can illustrate the operation of a liberal model of change with an example from the civil rights struggle in the United States. When faced with a challenge to change, the liberal model suggests that change be accepted, but that it be well-managed. Since social change is a fact of life, and since it does not alter the underlying system, it must simply be contained. In order to accomplish this task, it is important to identify the different interests within the black and white communities, securing the necessary changes without too dramatic a shaking of the structures. A stabilized resolution of the racial conflict is sought—not a basic transformation of the social system. In an attempt to pacify blacks with such reformist measures, advocates of the liberal model point to the amount of change that has already occurred and warn against change that is too rapid and too "revolutionary."

THE RADICAL MODEL

A third model of the dynamics of social change we will call the radical model. According to the radical perspective, society passes through different historical epochs like waves, with new forms emerging out of the contradictions of old forms. Old forms die and new ones appear. Fundamental systemic transformation occurs. The radical model is a *transformative/interdependent/participative* one; its basic metaphor is *artistic*. Let us look at each of these elements.

This model views social time as *transformative*. The traditional model sees society as unchanging, and the liberal model sees it as constantly progressing without changing its basic structures. But in the radical model, basic transformations occur in the very social structures, as the events of history bring about fundamentally new stages. There is a time linkage between past, present, and future, but it is a dialectical linkage whereby one stage emerges from another through a process of creative conflict.

According to this model, social space is *interdependent*. There is a systemic wholeness to society but of a quality that is different from the organic interrelationships of the traditional model. In the traditional model, the parts of society functioned together in organic harmony moving from phase to phase of a never-changing cycle. In the radical model, the interrelationship of the parts is creative or dialectical; conflicting forces come together to form totally new structures.

According to the radical interpretation of change, all parts of society are related to all other parts. Consequently a decision concerning any one part has implications for the whole. The rise of the price of oil affects the price of food. The amount of gasoline used by U.S. motorists affects and is affected by our foreign policy. The fashions of New York determine employment patterns in South Korea.

The governing principle of the radical model is *participative*. Recall that the traditional model left little room for participation, since society was governed by an authoritarian elite. The liberal model allowed participation, but because of contemporary societal complexities (compounded by individualism and competing interests), basic decisions were left in the hands of a managerial elite. The radical model, however, requires direct input from communities of ordinary people into the key decisions of our society—those in the political, economic, and cultural arenas. The "common good" is the consequence of cooperative participation by the people affected. The social virtue underlying this model is *community*.

The basic interpretative metaphor of the radical model is the work of art, or the act of *creation*. (For further elaboration on this idea, see Gibson Winter, *Liberating Creation: Foundations of Religious Social Ethics*, New York: Crossroad, 1981.) The artistic emphasis means that society is seen as a creative process, rather than a natural (traditional) or mechanistic (liberal) process. As a work of art, society is constructed in dialogue, shaped by community, and grows out of its members' dreams, myths, and visions. Such an emphasis opposes the bureaucratic management and administrative values of mature liberalism.

The radical model's stress on participation, creativity, and community also implies a different attitude toward conflict. The three interpretative models hold three fundamentally different attitudes toward conflict. For the traditional model, conflict is deviant and should be repressed. For the liberal model, conflict is superficial and merely requires management. However, for the radical model, conflict can be creative. The tensions produced by conflict are both the result of participation and the source of transformation. Hence, when faced with conflict in society, the radical response is to seek creative paths that lead to new and better forms of society—through fundamental structural transformation.

How has the radical model been manifest in the United States? Let us return to the example of racial conflict and the civil rights struggle. Guided by the radical model, an activist would take a much deeper structural approach to change than he or she would under the influence of a traditional or liberal model. According to the radical model, racism is not simply a personal prejudice, but a structural phenomenon, intimately related to the whole social system. That is, racism is incorporated into the economic, political, and cultural life of society. It is reflective of a system that increasingly makes large numbers of people irrelevant (e.g., the "urban underclass" in the United States that is predominantly black). Approaching this conflict from the perspective of the radical model, one would not repress the conflict, or simply manage it; rather, one would seek creative paths of transformation. The deepest structural roots of contemporary racism must be identified—in the economic, political, and cultural institutions of society—and efforts must be made to transform all structures.

Can we point to actual historical examples of the radical model of change? We think immediately of various revolutionary situations, wherein one political system was overthrown and another installed. Frequently, this political revolution was achieved by way of an economic revolution, in which a new system of organizing the economic functions of production and distribution was initiated. (Recall, for example, the Russian, Chinese, and Cuban Revolutions.) The radical changes that followed these revolutions occurred in basically agrarian societies. Moreover, in each instance, social conflict escalated to the level of armed struggle. The Soviet system ultimately became authoritarian, bureaucratic, and even repressive. (Some people make similar claims for Cuba and China, while others stress their social gains.)

For these reasons, the classical communist models have little appeal in advanced industrial societies. The social structure in such societies is more complex. Armed conflict seems absurd in an urbanized context where the slightest breakdown of electrical power, water system, etc., would cause devastating consequences, especially for the poor. It may be that we do not have any historical precedents for the transformation of advanced industrial capitalist societies. Hence, our task is not to copy other models, but to unleash our creative imagination.

EXAMPLES OF CHANGE

In sketching three different models for interpreting change, we have attempted to show how social analysis can clarify the responses taken to the challenge of social change and conflict. Although these models have relevance in concrete historical situations, reality is never as neat and precise as that presented here. Yet analysis of current situations according to these models—e.g., examining change in policies of the U.S. government, or change in practices of the church, etc.—can give us a deeper understanding of those situations.

Our choice of analytical models has particular relevance for pastoral planning for justice. What actions do we take? What do we support? Against what do we struggle? The traditional model emphasizes an organic approach which, in the face of conflict calls for *order*. The liberal model emphasizes a mechanistic approach which calls for *balance*. The radical model emphasizes an artistic approach which calls for *creativity*. We will now try to show what each of these models would mean with examples from international, domestic, and church experience.

International

Applying the three models of interpretation to recent international affairs, we can see some interesting contrasts in approaches to the global North/South conflict. The rich countries of the North are being confronted by the poor countries of the South, whose governments are demanding basic changes in international development. (In Chapter 3, we discuss the "development debate" in further detail.) Responses from the North vary markedly.

A traditional model guides a *confrontationist* or repressive response. No change whatsoever is considered necessary or acceptable in the rich/poor relationships of trade, aid, monetary arrangements, investments, political power, etc. In response to social unrest within poor countries, a traditionalist response would strengthen the police and military instruments to repress protesting social movements. Similarly, the basic international order is accepted and defended militarily. The future of the poor countries is either isolation or complete integration into the international system as it currently exists.

A blunt confrontationist stance can be seen in the actions of repressive military governments, frequently supported by the United States. Similarly, it has been present in U.S. international economic negotiations. During the Nixon presidency, Daniel Patrick Moynihan, then-U.S. ambassador to the United Nations, took a "hard line" approach to Third World problems. President Reagan and Jean Kirkpatrick followed a similar approach.

A liberal model guides an *accommodationist* response. Adherents to this model recognize that some change is called for—but not fundamental or systemic change. A smattering of adjustments in trade, aid, investments, etc., would assist the poor countries and counterbalance competing interests between rich and poor. The institution of an international "social welfare" program would be considered an adequate resolution of the problem.

In theory, such a program would allow for stabilization of the system and progress for all. The degree of change would be sufficient to keep the poor countries from "going under" in a drastic socio-economic collapse, but not sufficient to enable them to stand on their own with new-found strength. To some extent, this type of "conflict management" characterized the stance of the Carter Administration in its North/South negotiations, as well as that of its philosophical "mentor," the Trilateral Commission.

A radical model guides a *structuralist* response. According to this model, the root of the problems facing the poor countries can be found in the international economic order and in the national economic orders linked to it. No amount of "tinkering" with the current global order will remedy the situation. The rich/poor relationships need to be transformed through creative efforts to restructure the global social system. The call for a "New International Economic Order" (NIEO) is an instance of the structuralist response, though a more thorough response requires new national social orders as well. (For further elaboration, see Chapter 3.)

Domestic

Further application of these interpretative models can be seen in the recent politics of change in the United States. Take, for example, the responses to the challenge of poverty.

A traditional model represses the challenge from movements of the poor. Their demands for change are rejected; social structures are left as they are. "Blaming the victim" (i.e., the poor themselves) is commonplace. We are frequently reminded that "the poor you have always with you." Many conservative politicians espouse these lines. And the "neo-conservative" intellectual movement has tried to give it new respectability by speaking of the need to "lower expectations."

A liberal model acknowledges the need for some change so that the system can survive. It becomes a matter of balancing different interests, managing conflict that might otherwise become dangerous. Thus, urban development is designed to offer more jobs; "head-start" and remedial educations programs are begun in both urban and rural areas of poverty; and business is encouraged to provide on-the-job training. President Lyndon Johnson's "War on Poverty" was a significant liberal response to the socio-economic problems of the mid-1960s. Its rapid demise, however, raised serious questions, not only about the effectiveness of its programs, but also about the validity of the philosophy that motivated them.

A radical model sees within the system itself serious structural problems that cannot be remedied by slight adjustments. The cure is broad structural transformation. Capital and technology, for example, the twin engines of the economy, should be made directly accountable to community, controlled by the people affected by their use. The radical model perceives the problem to be, not the amount of industrialization or rate of growth, but the nature of production and distribution. The radical response to poverty in the United States has not been espoused by mainstream leaders, though it is being voiced by growing numbers of citizens. It gives rise to many suggestions of "alternative" approaches in economics, politics, and culture. (These new approaches will be discussed in more detail in Chapter 3.)

Church

Looking directly at the church, what would the application of these three models suggest? This topic obviously needs more extensive development; however, let us note at least a few points that have serious pastoral consequences.

A traditional model responds to the challenge of change within the church by re-emphasizing traditional categories of belief and practice. *Resistance* to change is a characteristic note. A static unchanging image of the church is projected, even in the terminology adopted (e.g., references to the "deposit of faith," the "state of grace," and "eternal truths"). Authority is stressed and orthodoxy equated with uniformity. Some of the reaction to Vatican II—e.g., by Bishop Lefebvre and his followers—can be interpreted through the analysis suggested by the traditional model.

A liberal model embraces the changes in the church, allowing progress to be made within the current structure. This process is called *renewal*. For example, liturgy is improved within the existing parish setting. A greater voice is given to pastoral councils within the dioceses. Wider apostolic opportunities are offered to religious, etc., but no fundamental transformation of ministry or structure occurs. This evolutionary change is the most common experience of the U.S. church in response to Vatican II.

A radical model seeks new ways of responding to the challenge of change within the church. *Re-creation* is the model, as the early church experience is examined to discover its relevance (in new forms) for today. Still taking shape within the church is the basic Christian community (*comunidad de base*) movement, a significant example of the restructuring of religious institutions. Within this movement, greater participation of ordinary people is sought; new lay ministries, perhaps even a restructuring of priesthood and religious orders, is beginning to take shape. New networks of communities are springing up, and linkages with movements for radical change in the wider society are being promoted.

SUMMARY / CONCLUSION

Change is going on around us all the time. The work for social justice is largely a work to direct that process toward a social situation more respectful of human rights and dignity. Thus, pastoral action that promotes justice needs to understand the dynamics of social change and relate creatively to those dynamics. In the preceding chapter, we sketched three interpretative models for understanding change and suggested some of the implications for the pastoral responses that flow from each model.

There are two complementary uses for a social analysis of models of change. *First*, analysis helps us to understand the responses taken by those in positions of influence and authority to a given social situation. When action on behalf of justice confronts opposition, it is important to examine the model of change employed by those who support the *status quo*. We can then sort out the various tactics and strategies necessary to move toward further change.

Each of the models has a particular "language" appropriate to it. Association of key catchwords with their appropriate change models will help us to determine the particular orientation of the individuals with whom we are dealing. For example, a person employing a traditional model will speak of "order," "proper lines of authority," and "the accepted way of doing things." Someone guided by a liberal model may prefer "balance," "both sides," "gradual development," and "the give-and-take of a process." Use of terms like "new order of things," "unprecedented," or "transformation" reveal more openness to a radical model.

Second, the models of change help us know our own strengths and weaknesses. If we examine our own experiences honestly—personal experiences as well as institutional experiences—we probably are aware that we operate according to *all* models of change. At different times, in differing situations, we tend to support actions that are "system preserving," or "system reforming," or "system transforming." This sort of "inconsistency" is understandable—and may even be desirable. There is a time to preserve tradition, a time for reform, and a time for basic transformation. But which time is it in the history of our social system? This question is one of discernment.

In any case, we need to be consciously aware of our choice and to identify our particular biases toward various models of change. Only by being so aware can we determine the effectiveness of our own stance toward the social reality that confronts us.

Perhaps the best way to appreciate the importance of a social analysis that seriously considers the dynamics of change is to apply it to concrete social situations that face us today. In Chapter 3, we will examine "change" as it relates to Third World and domestic "development," searching for models that suggest practical pastoral responses to a rapidly changing world.

Chapter 3

The Development Debate: Its Wider Implications

Again, the way in which a problem is defined determines to a large extent the range of solutions we might propose. Take, for example, a bright teenager who is having learning difficulties in a classroom situation. If the problem is defined simply as tiredness, we might recommend more sleep or extra vitamins. However, if we determine that the student has seeing and hearing problems, we would propose glasses and a hearing aid. However, if we define the problem as one of teacher hostility toward this particular student, we might suggest the pupil change to another classroom. Definitions of social problems have similar consequences in terms of the responses that we choose. Social analysis helps us sort out those definitions.

To illustrate the usefulness of social analysis in this regard, we will look at three *"models"* of *international development* and explore the implications of each for problems on the domestic scene and for the pastoral responses of religious groups.

Why do we pick the broad topic of international development to illustrate this particular approach to social analysis? First, it is a topic that the Center of Concern has probed in a variety of ways over the past several years. Hence, it is an area that we know well, and one we have found to have many wider implications. Second, international development, according to the models we have chosen, is a topic that directly parallels various processes occurring in the United States and in the church. A better understanding of these models can enhance our performance of pastoral action for social justice.

COMPETING MODELS OF DEVELOPMENT

What do we mean when we speak of the problem of "development" at the international level? It has become increasingly obvious that there are few problems more critical in our world than that of world poverty. The world's present population—over four billion people—will double before 2020. Ninety percent of that increase will occur in the poor nations of Africa, Asia, and Latin America. World Bank estimates indicate that close to one billion people—nearly one out of every four—live in subhuman conditions of hunger, sickness, illiteracy, inadequate shelter, and unclean drinking water. They exist without hope. Although the global situation is improving in some regions, it is growing even more dismal for an increasing number of people.

How are we to analyze this international picture of poverty and misery? First, we must define the term "development." For our purposes, we have chosen three interpretative models (see p. 48, Chart B).

Economic

The economic model, the one that continues to dominate most of the established development thinking and planning in the world today, analyzes the situation in terms of *capitalization*. Lack of capital is considered to be the major problem in the Third World. According to this model, societies are underdeveloped because they do not have investments sufficient to stimulate new production, generate jobs, finance research, or promote consumption. Operating according to this definition, development planners prescribe the infusion of new capital—through international aid programs, foreign investment, technical assistance, etc.—as a remedy for underdevelopment. In order to boost the gross national product (GNP—the sum of a nation's goods and services), they seek an increase in economic growth. Heavy industrial production is particularly emphasized.

The economic model provides the criteria that determine which countries are "developed" and which are "developing" (or "underdeveloped," "less developed," etc.). For example, the United States, with a GNP per capita of over $7000 is considered to be "developed." However, India, with a GNP per capita of only $150, is "developing."

CHART B
DEVELOPMENT MODELS AND IMPLICATIONS

Model:	Economic (1960s)	Social (1970s)	Political (1980s)
Economics:	Capitalization	Distribution	Transformation
Politics:	Stability	Aid	Mobilization
Culture:	Growth	Equity	Imagination
Transportation:	More Cars and Highways	More Purchasing Power	Mass Transit Systems
Health:	More Technology	Better Distribution of Services	Alternative Health Systems
Housing:	More Construction	Rent Control	Community Planning
Missions:	Vocations from the Middle Class	Work with the Poor	New Forms of Lay Ministry
U.S. Economic Crisis:	More Capital Formation and Consumer Austerity	Increased Regulation, Expansion of Social Welfare State.	Alternative Economic Structures

---

In the economic model, the focus of discussion is national. Consequently, the structural difficulties impeding development are considered to be internal to the developing nation (e.g., lack of savings, poor management, inefficient technology). Its political remedy is authoritarian; political "stability" that protects investments, not structural change, is called for. "Stability," of course, is a code word for dictatorship and repression. Behind such responses lies a traditional ideology.

Social

The economic model relies heavily on the measurements of GNP per capita to indicate the level of development within a given country. However, it ignores a major component of social analysis—*distribution*. What actually happens to the benefits accrued from the growing economy? Who is actually enjoying these benefits? As we entered the decade of the 1970s, such questions increasingly came to the fore. Why was it that countries like Mexico, Brazil, and India, whose rates of GNP per capita were higher than those of many developing countries, continued to be marked by widespread poverty?

The analysis suggested by the social model of development defines the problem, not as a lack of capital, but as the "marginality" of the poor due to inadequate distribution of resources. In many countries, large numbers of the population remain marginalized from the growing economy, neither contributing to it nor benefiting from it. In fact, 40 percent or more of the population of many developing countries remains very poor; most of the benefits of development flow to a small elite at the top of the social scale.

In response to this problem, proponents of the social model attempt to spread the benefits of growth more evenly—especially through income redistribution schemes (e.g., tax reforms, wage increases, improved public services, etc.). The major focus of the response is again within the national boundaries of the developing country. A liberal ideology or social welfare approach marks this model; its goal is the redistribution of wealth within the present system.

Political

The third model of development, a political model, moves the analysis of Third World poverty beyond the issues of capitalization and distribution, toward the *transformation* of the total system. According to this model, the underdevelopment of the Third World is rooted in historically-generated structures of "dependency." This analysis implies that improvement in the lives of the majority of people is blocked—both internally and externally—by individuals and groups who benefit from the present concentration of power.

At the international level, colonial patterns of political domination have been replaced by neo-colonial patterns of economic domination—e.g., unequal trade arrangements, the investment practices of multinational corporations, monetary manipulation, etc. At the national level, wealthy elites in both the developed and developing countries help each other to reinforce their dominance over the majority of the people. The political model is particularly concerned with the redistribution of power—and the structural changes that such a transfer entails.

As suggested by the political model, development efforts should not focus exclusively on the *quantitative* aspects of economic growth—either on the amount of wealth generated or its pattern of distribution. Rather, the focus should be on the *quality* of growth that is occurring. Upon whose terms is the economy structured? By what values is it guided? What are the structural consequences of the present arrangement? At the international level, the political model stresses the transformation of North/South relationships through a New International Economic Order (NIEO). At the national level, it stresses a societal transformation from a "profit system" to a "needs system," founded in structures that generate employment and promote community participation.

According to the political model, the locus of the problem is global. That is, the chief impediments to the development of all people are power elites, backed by economic, political, and cultural structures on both the national and international levels. The ideology of the model can be termed "radical," in the sense that it goes to the *root* of the problem, emphasizing structural transformation.

In the early 1960s, the *capitalization* analysis governed much of the rich world's response to the poor world's need. Massive aid programs were initiated to industrialize developing nations' economies. In the late 1960s and early 1970s, faced with the recognition that the benefits of the economic model were not "trickling down" to the impoverished masses, a *distribution* analysis suggested new approaches. Development aid began to focus on women, the rural sector of the economy, etc.—rather than on heavy industrial projects. In the second half of the 1970s, the focus of the Third World began to shift to a *transformation* analysis, calling for a complementary restructuring of both the global and domestic orders. But in most cases, the dominant national and international groups in both the First and Third Worlds will not be the leaders of such a transformation.

At this point, we can see the importance of social analysis in identifying problems. Depending upon the definition offered by our analysis of the development problem, we will emphasize one set of policies over another and certain social groups over others. The economic model, for example, looks to business leaders to increase capitalization. The social model, by contrast, looks to technocrats to design new schemes to balance various social and economic forces. The political model, however, looks to grassroots social movements, especially among the poor, to mount the challenge to society.

In sum, it is insufficient to lament the global miseries of hunger, poverty, and oppression. It is similarly insufficient to urge "let's do something!" We need adequate analysis to pinpoint the deepest roots of the problem and to shape the most effective response.

DOMESTIC IMPLICATIONS

Our analyses of Third World problems can give us insight into the domestic problems that face us in the United States. Once again, the competing development models offer different analytical definitions of the problems and suggest different approaches for their resolution.

Take, for example, the *transportation* situation in most large urban areas across our country. People must travel from home to work, school, shops, recreation areas, etc. As anyone living in a large urban area knows, such transportation is becoming increasingly difficult and expensive.

How are we to understand the problem of urban transportation? The application of the social analysis found in the models of development provides a few insights. The first analysis (capitalization) would stress the need to generate more capital in order to produce more automobiles and construct more freeways. The second analysis (distribution) would reply that such an approach is inappropriate if people cannot afford to own and operate cars. Consequently, this analysis would stress the need to increase workers' wages, give tax benefits to the lower and middle class, and perhaps design a guaranteed income plan for the poor. All of these programs would distribute income more widely, thus increasing people's opportunity to own and operate a car.

The third analysis (transformation) would point out that a new set of problems has been created as a result of the energy shortage and air pollution. Taking these factors into account, the third analysis would prescribe neither more private automobiles and highways, nor more income with which to buy them, but a new mass transit system designed to meet everyone's needs. In effect, the third analysis calls for a significant transformation of the whole structure of transportation—for a creative effort to construct new systems to meet new challenges.

Another application of these models can be found in our *health system*. Sophisticated medical technology has enabled people to live longer. Many diseases and accidents that took large tolls in the past—e.g., tuberculosis, polio, heart attacks, broken bones, etc.—are now treated routinely. Yet, there are still serious health problems in the United States, heightened by both poverty and affluence. How can we respond creatively to these problems?

The capitalization analysis would stress the need for building up the "capital" of health care: more doctors, technology, and hospitals. Money for research would be sought and new construction undertaken at the great medical centers across the country. The distribution analysis would urge that the number of health centers be increased, and that doctors be encouraged to practice in small towns, rural areas, and poorer sections of the inner-city. Improved medical benefits and insurance programs would be made available to an even greater number of people.

The transformation analysis calls for a more thorough review of the health field. According to this analysis, the problem is not simply a matter of technological inadequacies or poor distribution of services. The transformation analysis raises serious questions about the structure and quality of health care in the United

States. The problems will not be solved until these structures are transformed—until there is a holistic, preventive, deprofessionalized, and community-controlled health program. Cancer, for example, will not be cured until it is rooted out at the source, namely, radioactive waste, industrial pollution, food additives, etc.—an act that requires a radical transformation of society.

Finally, in the field of domestic *housing*, the United States faces a serious crisis. The housing situation is grim for middle-income people, let alone for the poor. According to the first analysis, more capital is needed to build new housing units and renovate old ones. The second analysis suggests that better distribution of existing facilities is required—through such mechanisms as rent control, lower mortgage rates, housing subsidies for low-income families, etc. The third analysis explores the structural elements of the housing problem and determines that the entire housing system must be transformed. Included in such a change would be large-scale community planning for housing needs, community control over the capital acquired, and new housing designs based on social and natural ecology.

The competing models of development offer different analyses of other domestic problems as well. Think, for instance, of our food system (agribusiness versus small farmers; chemical farming versus organic farming), education system (especially, quality education issues), the emergence of a permanent underclass of unemployed youth, the cybernetic revolution of microprocessors, etc. The models of development obviously have implications that extend far beyond the bounds of the international arena.

PASTORAL IMPLICATIONS

As we bring the discussion of competing development models to the level of pastoral planning, we are faced with two specific challenges: (1) to design missionary strategies abroad; and (2) to deal with socioeconomic tensions at home. Social analysis is required in both instances—in order to avoid mistakes and to make the best use of scarce resources. The capitalization, distribution, and transformation analyses will help us to understand the experiences of many U.S. religious groups over the past two decades.

Designing Missionary Strategies

Since the early 1960s, the Catholic Church in the United States, along with various Protestant churches, has shown increasing interest in Latin America. Challenged by the concurrent rise of communism, Protestantism, and secularism in Latin America, Catholic Church leaders looked for a new way to respond.

The initial pastoral response was strongly influenced by a capitalization analysis. Why was the classic Catholic ecclesial strategy no longer working in Latin America? The first answer given was simple: a lack of sufficient "clerical capital" (priests, religious). Thus, the primary solution was the generation or infusion of new clergy. Since native vocations were not immediately forthcoming, clergy from the outside were recruited. Hundreds of priests, religious, and lay personnel went from the United States to Latin America to help "develop" the local church. They generally supported the middle class, hoping to cultivate a source of future vocations. Schools and hospitals were built and staffed; whole dioceses were furnished with clergy and bishops.

Nonetheless, it soon became clear that the clerical capital had to move beyond the middle class to the poor, who made up the majority of the church in Latin America. The new analysis suggested a new pastoral strategy. It was not enough to evangelize the middle class with the hope that it would produce the new vocations—vocations who would finally share the gospel with the rest of society. Rejecting this "trickle down" theory, missionaries began to go directly to the poor. Otherwise, the poor would be lost and no later generation of middle class native vocations could retrieve them.

Thus began the shift to a pastoral response influenced by a distribution analysis. Priests, sisters, brothers, and lay religious professionals began a dramatic attempt to cross class lines and identify themselves with the poor. Sometimes they worked in official ministerial roles, sometimes simply in ministries of presence. The poor welcomed the missionaries and responded to their ministerial initiatives. The middle class church, from which the missionaries came, also gained—learning of social worlds from which it had previously been insulated. The church began to develop new insights into the injustices of past and present society—with significant consequences for what we now call the "Medellín Church" (after the 1968 Conference of Latin American Bishops).

The extent to which the new ministry actually affected the poor needs critical evaluation. Important changes were indeed made, but in most cases, the small changes that resulted from years of devoted effort were overwhelmed by the events of the growing crisis. Only now are the deepest questions being raised, involving a new strategy based upon a new analysis.

This new approach is based upon the transformation analysis. It sees the need to transform the nature of ministry and the structures of the traditional church. While trained religious professionals (the capitalization model) and the broad sharing of their services (the distribution model) are still required, a whole new model of the church (basic Christian communities) and a new model of ministry (perhaps lay priests ordained directly from the poor themselves) are also desperately needed.

For example, the Aymara Indians of the Altiplano of Bolivia have welcomed the work of the professional religious personnel who have come to them from the First World, and they will continue to welcome them. Yet, the task of evangelization will not be finished until one day a church is built that blends such professional ministers with indigenous lay pastors—ordained in the fullest sense to preach the gospel and minister the sacraments. These lay pastors will probably include married people—both men and women. Most important, however, they may not be university or seminary graduates, but community religious leaders, guided by in-service training from religious professionals. Such a rooted lay ministry would mean a genuine transformation of current missionary strategy.

Religious groups that send missionaries to Latin America (or to other parts of the Third World) need to ask the deeper questions that stem from social analysis. While the questions themselves will not solve the problems, they can help to formulate the plan for transformation. The transformation analysis reflects most accurately the new direction of the church in Latin America. The training, life style, apostolic work, and spirituality of the missionaries will all be affected. Thus, we begin to see its pastoral planning consequences.

Facing Socio-Economic Tensions

The second challenge to religious groups is closer to home. Since the 1970s, United States society has been involved in a deepening economic crisis. As a result of increasing inflation, religious groups are facing serious problems with institutional finances. The impact of the crisis is manifest in all aspects of life: in rising fuel and food bills; in growing medical costs for the aged; in higher fees for the services of Catholic schools and hospitals; in the desire of these same institutions to avoid salary increases, while they are increasingly confronted by the organizing drives of labor unions.

What is happening? With what strategy can religious groups respond? As we have seen, the analysis that we choose defines both the problem and the consequent pastoral response.

The capitalization analysis is regularly championed by the business community in the United States. It is written into the pages of the *Wall Street Journal* and *Business Week* and in the advertisements of Mobil, IBM, Chase Manhattan, and other large corporations and financial institutions. The definition of the problem, according to this interpretation, is capital shortage. Thus, the policy response is capital formation.

In other words, the capitalization analysis holds that the economy is not productive enough because entrepreneurs do not have sufficient investment funds to build new plants and develop new technology, which in turn would create more jobs and greater production, with consequent growth and prosperity. How do we meet this challenge? Through public policy designed to give more tax incentives to big business, hold down wages, reduce spending in the public sector (libraries, schools, hospitals, social services, etc.), reduce consumer spending, raise interest rates, and control the money supply.

While this model is attractive to the business community, its critics claim that such policies would precipitate deeper class conflict in American society, downward mobility for the middle class, greater exploitation of the working class, and incredible hardship for the poor.

The distribution analysis, promoted by social welfare liberals, provides a second response to the current economic crisis. Social welfare liberals would increase, rather than decrease, public spending in order to stimulate employment. They would give tax incentives to ordinary people, reduce interest rates and increase the money supply, and allow wages to rise with inflation. They argue that by increasing purchasing power, and thus generating demand, supply will also increase. This response, typical of "Keynesian" thinking (named for economist Lord Maynard Keynes), has guided the United States' economy since the New Deal. Critics of this model maintain that the United States is in the midst of a new structural stage, situated in a new structural environment. The capital-intensive technological period and the more competitive world market have rendered social liberal solutions obsolete. (See Chapter 4 for further elaboration.)

The transformation analysis represents a third response to the economic crisis. According to this analysis, the current economic crisis is deeper than either a capitalization or a distribution analysis suggests. Our economy, this analysis argues, has basic structural problems—highly concentrated corporate and government power, an increasingly unregulated transnational movement of capital, energy-intensive technology, structural unemployment and structural inflation, etc. These problems require the creation of alternative social structures.

One transformation analysis, the product of the Exploratory Project for Economic Alternatives (Washington, D.C.), argues that the worst inflation occurs in the basic necessities—food, energy, health, and housing. Inflation in the necessities particularly affects the poor. Rather than adjusting existing structures, we must explore alternatives in the sub-systems of food, energy, health, and housing—i.e., food cooperatives, health care cooperatives, community energy-saving arrangements, cooperative housing, etc.

According to each of these three social analyses, what strategies are open to Christian communities that seek to meet the current U.S. economic and social crisis?

The first analysis would suggest that the Christian community identify its interests with those of large business corporations, pushing for a public policy that would tighten the economy and cut back on social programs. However, the religious concern for the poor stands in direct opposition to such a choice!

The second analysis suggests that Christians lobby for more effective social welfare legislation within the present system and side with those who suffer most from the current crisis. This response appears both necessary and worthwhile, but it does not of itself address the structural causes of the problem.

The third analysis suggests the creative exploration of alternative structures. In an effort to transform our society, from one based primarily on production for profit and consumption toward one based on meeting basic human needs and defending fundamental human rights, religious groups could play a significant role. For example, churches maintain a considerable number of social institutions and control many social services oriented to human needs (i.e., schools, hospitals, charitable programs, community organizations, etc.). A social analysis of the urban crisis in the large cities of the Northeast might suggest creative recommitments to educating the poor about the structural roots of their suffering. Or, a social analysis of rural areas in the Midwest and South might encourage a movement to maintain small family farms or suggest the institution of agricultural cooperatives against the advance of giant agribusiness operations.

Once we begin to think in terms of transformation, our "creative imagination" is freed. For instance, a religious community housed in a semi-rural setting might want to experiment with producing its own food, perhaps in an organic farming cooperative, and generating some of its own energy through wind and solar technologies. These experiments could, in turn, become models for wider social application, just as the early Benedictine monasteries served as agricultural experimentation centers, helping to rebuild Western civilization after the barbarian invasions.

Another example, perhaps more suitable for urban-based groups, would be the establishment of a "development bank," focusing on alternative structures designed to meet basic human needs. By creating such a bank, and depositing a percentage of their investments in it, these groups could provide working capital for alternative social projects—e.g., urban housing cooperatives, community health centers, food and fuel cooperatives, etc.—that would not otherwise be possible. (See adjoining article on alternative investments.) Such experiments in alternative investments complement the efforts of many religious groups to encourage "corporate responsibility" within existing economic structures.

Is it "utopian" to think of creating alternative social and economic structures? To answer this question realistically, we must ask what other paths are open to religious groups that wish to respond effectively to our growing social crisis.

The social analyses suggested by the three competing models of development point to diverse paths. One, promoting only capitalization, is religiously unacceptable; another, adding distribution, is admirable but insufficient; the third, transformation, is potentially the most far-reaching. Hence, pastoral planning needs to explore alternative ways of maintaining present institutional commitments, as well as new patterns of response that may mean the abandonment of some contemporary institutions. If either avenue is ignored, our institutional response to the current social crisis could increase, rather than decrease, human suffering.

SUMMARY/CONCLUSION

In this chapter, we have analyzed various definitions of development, examining each one in terms of its particular strategic response. Internationally, the problem of development has been regarded primarily as *economic*—the lack of sufficient capital; or primarily as *social*—the lack of sufficient distribution; or primarily as *political*—the lack of structural transformation. Each of these models contains elements of truth; aspects of all of them are included in every social analysis. One model, however, is always dominant.

Thus, while we have noted the application of these analytical models to domestic issues such as transportation, health, and housing, we must always be cautious of oversimplification. In most real-world situations, there will be a need for additional capital and more equitable distribution. However, the third analysis challenges us to examine the structures that promote underdevelopment and encourages us to find a means to transform them. To stop short of asking such fundamental questions is to face current challenges with a superficial understanding and response.

For groups engaged in pastoral planning for social justice action, these competing models of development can serve as effective stimuli for deeper reflection and stronger action. Regarding the utilization of their resources, religious groups make decisions according to their definitions of the problems that face them. Whether it be missionary activities overseas or pastoral responses in the United States, the social analysis suggested in these models invites religious groups to pay closer attention to the transformation of structures, rather than to the maintenance of existing ones.

APPENDIX TO CHAPTER 3:
ALTERNATIVE INVESTMENTS
IN BASIC HUMAN NEEDS

by Joe Holland

A social analysis of the economic situation in the United States suggests a strategy of alternative investments. The following article explores the implications of this response. (An expanded version of this article appeared in New Catholic World, *Vol. 222, No. 1329, May/June, 1979. It has been reprinted with the permission of Paulist Press.)*

There is substantial investment money in the religious community. Insurance policies, pension funds, stock portfolios for churches or religious orders, savings to pay for children's college—all of these are investment capital. What is a Christian use of these funds?

At present there are two main ways of responding to this question. Some respond in the form of *divestment*, or giving it away, in order to pursue a more simple lifestyle. Others follow the path of *corporate responsibility* by pressuring corporations, where funds are invested, to be ethical. Both of these responses are good. I would like to explore, however, a third way which might be pursued instead of these or in conjunction with them. I call this response *alternative investments in basic human needs*. But before getting into it, it may be helpful to review the other two and see why an additional response is called for.

Divestment, the first response, could be called the Franciscan way, but it goes back to Jesus himself. Time and again he taught us not to worry about tomorrow and about money. Our heavenly Father, he said, would care for us like lilies of the field. In American Catholicism, the Catholic Worker Movement under the inspiration of Dorothy Day has kept this response alive. We all owe a great debt to her saintly witness and to the entire Catholic Worker family. But while this response captures one dimension of Jesus' call, it is not the full answer. For one thing, it often reflects an anarchist interpretation of society, which not all Christians share. For another, while directly ministering to the poor and identifying with them, it may not get to the structural roots of poverty and oppression.

Corporate responsibility is the second response. This is the opposite of an anarchist approach. Instead, it tries to influence gigantic corporate economic structures by research, public disclosure, and stockholder pressure. This response has been applied by many religious groups over issues like affirmative action, apartheid in South Africa, and the infant formula issue in the Third World. Many who follow this strategy do not accept the legitimacy of autonomous corporate bodies, but use the strategy to educate the public and make immediate pragmatic gains. Again this is an important contribution, complementing the divestment response, but it too has shortcomings. Basically it accepts the social and technological framework as we have it.

The third response, which I am suggesting here, is not a substitute for the other two, nor one which is superior to them. Rather it is only one more response, alongside the other two, to be appraised and tested by different groups, depending on their particular charisms and guidance in the Spirit.

A modern society is shaped by how its capital is invested. If the decision is made to invest huge amounts of capital in petroleum energy and the private automobile, you get a society marked by the suburban sprawl which grew up after World War II. If the decision were made instead to invest in solar energy and a mass transit system as our basic transportation grid, we would have a very different kind of society. Similarly if the decision were made to heavily finance neighborhood health clinics and cooperative housing, we would have different housing and health structures.

In our country the top decision makers who decide how the

country should be structured—that is, those who control the main direction of capital and technology—are probably only one percent of the population. Chase Manhattan Bank recently ran a full page ad in *The New York Times*, beginning: "When your finances place you among the top one percent. . . ." This is the group who shapes the country. Obviously the Soviet Union has its top one percent as well, even though they are in the public sector rather than the private sector. People can quarrel about the strengths and weaknesses of having your top one percent of decision makers in the public or private sectors. But I think most would agree that in neither system do *communities of ordinary people* have much voice. I can't imagine, for example, that the ordinary people of either country, after a thoughtful debate, would decide to invest so much capital and technological energy in the arms race. But what chance do communities of ordinary people have to shape such basic investment decisions?

What is surprising is that most of the capital in our society already belongs to ordinary people. Rich people and rich institutions certainly have a great deal of their own, but not enough to account for their disproportionate power. Actually they are powerful because they *control the capital of others*. Thus when we pay the premiums on our insurance policies, send off our monthly mortgage checks, make our pension payments, and send off our tax bill, we are handing over to other decision makers the basic working capital of the country. It is the capital of ordinary people which is then controlled by large corporate bureaucracies and invested in ways which increasingly fail to meet the basic human needs of ordinary people, including sometimes those whose money it was.

An ecumenical religious coalition in Youngstown, Ohio, for example, both morally and politically tried to challenge the idea that a company has no accountability to the community in which it is located. In that case, Youngstown Sheet and Tube Company, a steel plant, was absorbed by the Lykes Corporation, a large conglomerate, and its facilities were closed to generate capital for other uses. As a result, thousands of workers and their families were left unemployed, with a ripple effect throughout the region. Yet it was the labor of those workers, and also the capital of ordinary people, which helped build the industry in the first place.

What relevance has all this for the Christian community in the United States? I suggest that the religious community could begin some important experiments precisely in this area. Many religious orders, for example, maintain large retirement funds for their elderly. They cannot give it away, since that would abandon their aged. Trying to be responsible, the most they can do is pressure large corporations to be ethical; but that does not meet the basic human needs of people. Some groups, therefore, might begin to experiment, even with a small portion of their funds, to make financing available for meeting basic human needs through worker or consumer community cooperatives.

An example would be to make retirement funds available for cooperative housing (without a down payment) for responsible low income families to buy or build their own homes.

Perhaps it would be better if several congregations pooled a percentage of their funds in a single experiment. If it worked, and if they found ways to manage it professionally with a reasonable return, it might then be expanded. They might also look for innovative areas, stressing alternative technologies, like solar energy.

Groups besides religious orders could take part in this experiment. Parish churches might be willing to lend money to such a capital pool. Middle-class couples with modest savings, for retirement or college for the children, could also allot capital to the pool. If the initiative were to spread widely across religious institutions, it could eventually become a very significant capital pool.

Groups might even want to consider establishing a board of directors or advisors made up heavily of poor people, to set policy for the body. The U.S. Catholic bishops' Campaign for Human Development is a good example of how to involve the poor themselves in the decision-making process.

Of course such an experiment would not totally change our social structures. However, it would teach people that the structures of society do not fall down from heaven, but are the product of human decision. Opening up people's imagination, while not of itself bringing change, might be a key step toward it.

Chapter 4

Industrialization
and Pastoral Responses

Key to the previous three chapters has been the insight that pastoral action always responds to a specific social context. This social context should be carefully analyzed if we are to make adequate pastoral responses. Various approaches to social analysis have been explained and exemplified as tools of pastoral action.

In this chapter, we offer one particular analysis of the national and international social context today. We then suggest some of the implications for church pastoral response, particularly, the Catholic Church. We offer the analysis for two reasons: (1) it provides one comprehensive explanation of a variety of social factors and dynamics today; and (2) it provides an example of what social analysis can do—pointing to historical and structural elements of the reality in which we are immersed and in which we are planning pastoral responses.

The following analysis is a summary of a larger study developed by Joe Holland, which will be published in the near future. We include the material here because many groups have, through various workshops and lectures, found this overview helpful and its implications challenging.

THE STAGES OF INDUSTRIAL CAPITALISM

According to our analysis, the fundamental social context challenging the contemporary church is the process of *industrializa-*

tion. In the West, industrialization has taken the form of capitalism, sometimes referred to as "liberalism." The roots of this process go back centuries to the decline of the Middle Ages, the emergence of modern science, the formation of capital, the consolidation of nation states, the rise of the great cities, and the creation of modern social classes. Our particular focus is the process of industrialization originally in nineteenth- and twentieth-century Western Europe and the United States—now expanded to the Third World—that is, the formation of "industrial capitalism."

In the twentieth century, we have also seen the development of communist forms of industrialization. Critical reflections could also be made about these forms. However, they are not part of our immediate context. Nor have they been decisive factors in the strategic responses of the church until the period following the Second World War.

In our analysis of industrial capitalism and the church's strategic responses, we will make use of two detailed charts:

> *Chart C, "Three Stages of Industrial Capitalism"*
> *Chart D, "Three Strategic Pastoral Responses"*

For analytical purposes, we have divided the history of industrialization into three historical structural stages or periods, each with a distinct internal dynamic. (1) The first stage is *laissez-faire* industrial capitalism, developing throughout the nineteenth century. (2) The second stage is *social welfare* industrial capitalism, taking shape since the turn of the twentieth century, coming to fruition in the United States with the "New Deal" of Franklin Delano Roosevelt. The conclusion of this stage coincided, more or less, with the end of Lyndon Johnson's presidency at the close of the 1960s. (3) The third stage is *national security* industrial capitalism, germinating throughout the post-World War II period, and emerging as a distinct period in the last third of the twentieth century. Richard Nixon was the first American president to preside over this third stage of industrial capitalism.

As shown in Chart C, each of these stages is analyzed in terms of its structural and functional parts. There are two "deep structures" in each stage—the structure of *capital* and the structure of *technology.* Moreover, there are different "functional regions" —*economic, political,* and *cultural*—each of which is conditioned by the deep structures.

The transitions between the various stages of capitalism are not abrupt and total shifts. Rather, they are the result of processes that have been evolving over decades, and they are often uneven in their development. Similarly, the decline of one stage overlaps with the rise of the next, and there is considerable ambiguity throughout. Finally, it is important to bear in mind that these analytical pictures are abstract crosscuts of reality. As such, they

CHART C
THREE STAGES OF INDUSTRIAL CAPITALISM

	I *Laissez-Faire* *Industrial Capitalism* *(Nineteenth Century)*	*II* *Social Welfare* *Industrial Capitalism* *(1900–1968)*	*III* *National Security* *Industrial Capitalism* *(1968–?)*
Deep Structures:			
Capital:	Local (Family firm)	National (Corporation)	Transnational (Conglomerate)
Technology:	Labor-Intensive	Capital/Labor Balance	Capital-Intensive
Functional Regions:			
Economic:	Exploitation; Austerity; Class Conflict	Strong Unions; Prosperity; Social Contract.	Exploitation and Marginalization; New Austerity; Community vs. Centralized Power.
Political:	Minimal State	Regulatory State	Authoritarian State
Cultural:	Freedom as License for the Few (Libertarian Liberalism)	Freedom as Opportunity for the Many (Social Liberalism)	Freedom as Security for the Few (Conservative Liberalism)

exclude the complexity present in any historical period. Nonetheless, these pictures help to focus on the most important elements of each period and point out key questions that must be confronted in each of the historical stages.

It is our thesis that our present social context represents a third stage of industrial capitalism, and that this stage is fundamentally different from the second stage, during which most of us grew up. The preceding statement is extremely important. It implies that since this stage is new, the pastoral strategies that respond to it need also be new. This is not to say that past strategies were bad. Quite the contrary. We are challenged to live up to the creativity of the pastoral strategies in earlier stages, but our response will be different, precisely because our context is different.

THE FIRST STAGE

The first stage of industrial capitalism and the hardening of the Catholic traditionalist strategy developed during the nineteenth century. Europe was its primary locus, although the United States, newly emerging as a nation, was significantly affected as well.

Laissez-Faire Industrial Capitalism

The first stage, *laissez-faire* industrial capitalism, was a brutal stage. Its very name, the French term for "let it be," was indicative of the lack of restrictions on monopoly, profit, and exploitative labor practices. The vivid portrayals in the novels of Charles Dickens provide literary reflection on the brutality of life in England during this period. Long working hours, unsafe conditions, poor pay, child labor, etc.—these were the daily hardships for the workers. However, in spite of the hardships, many people maintained a sense of hope—a belief that things would get better, if not for them, at least for their children.

In fact, things *did* get better for many. From 1840 on, per capita income in the United States doubled every forty-three years, and at least some of this increase "trickled down" to the workers. However, it is important to note that the situation improved, not simply because *laissez-faire* industrial capitalism reformed itself, but largely because a second, and more benevolent stage was taking shape within its womb.

The first stage of industrial capitalism had such brutal consequences, not because a bad generation of leaders presided over it, but because of structural elements intrinsic to the stage. These elements, the two deep structures, were the structures of capital and technology (see Chart C, column I).

First, *capital* during this first stage was, for the most part, locally based, operating in the form of numerous highly-competitive family firms. A classic example of this type of capital is the textile industry of the nineteenth century. As a consequence of the localized and competitive structure of this industry, benevolent management was punished and exploitative management rewarded. Benevolent entrepreneurs who attempted to pay the full social costs of production (e.g., decent wages) found their goods entering the market at higher prices than those of more ruthless competitors. The benevolent entrepreneurs were thus forced to change their managerial style, or they went bankrupt. Workers suffered terribly as a result. They worked long hours for low pay in unsanitary and dangerous conditions. The cheap labor of women and children served to further deflate the wages of male workers, who were forced to work for less pay or lose their jobs. Trade unions were generally repressed, and bloody labor wars were waged.

The structure of *technology* during this first stage of capitalism was a second major cause of the brutality of the period. Technology during this era was labor-intensive; that is, it consumed more labor than machinery (i.e., capital). Although slowly advancing, technology remained rudimentary and productivity low. As a result, the goods produced were not enough to create a consumer society. The few early automobiles, for example, served as "horseless carriages" for the wealthy. If the fruit of early automobile production had been divided evenly among the workers, one would have received a tire, another a steering wheel, and another a seat. There were simply not enough cars to go around.

Of course, production could have been designed with the intention of meeting the basic needs of the vast majority, but such a design was impossible without the guidance of some agency steering the economy according to a vision of the "common good." During the first stage of industrial capitalism, there was no such agency. The early liberal culture had become so individualistic that such holistic planning was culturally impossible. *Laissez-faire* was indeed the ruling ideology.

During this period, the three functional regions of society—economics, politics, and culture—were conditioned by the deep structures of capital and technology operative at the time.

Economic life during the *laissez-faire* period was difficult. Labor was in great demand, but working conditions were marked by severe exploitation, and consumer life was austere. However, these bleak conditions were set against a horizon of hope for a better future.

Karl Marx and the early socialist movements completely misunderstood this point. In the 1850s, Marx wrote that the longest span during which capitalism could survive was, at most, another fifty years. For this judgment, he was viewed by many radicals as "selling out" the imminent revolution. Today, however, we know that industrial capitalism was only warming up. More than a century later, it is still going strong.

Political life in the first stage of capitalism took the form of a minimalist state. The state intervened very little in the economy and assumed almost no responsibility for the general social welfare. As a result of this prevailing attitude, the first stage was called the era of *laissez-faire*—a time when the elites bowed to the "laws" of the marketplace. No matter what the consequences, they simply "let it be."

A classic and tragic example of the *laissez-faire* economy was the mid-nineteenth century Irish potato famine. When the potato crop (the staple food of the poor) failed, the British government refused to direct the still-flourishing cash crops of corn, wheat, and livestock from the export arena back to domestic consumption. Instead, following the principle of *laissez-faire,* the government allowed the food to go abroad where it commanded a higher price than the desperately poor Irish peasants could offer. Fifty percent of the population either fled the country or died. In this case, and in many others, the casualties of the social and economic system were left to private charity. In fact, many

Catholic religious congregations and charitable organizations were formed at this time, precisely in response to this kind of need.

As for *cultural* life, the central theme during this period was that of "freedom"—as indeed it remained throughout the succeeding stages of industrial capitalism. In the first stage, freedom had a negative definition—in two senses. First, it connoted freedom *from* the tradition of the past, or *historical* freedom. Second, it meant freedom *from* the restraints of the "common good," or *structural* freedom. Hence, early liberal freedom took the form of entrepreneurial license for the few, who pursued their goals with both personal autonomy and social recklessness. The philosophy of these early liberals was called "libertarianism."

Pastoral Response: The Traditionalist Strategy

The church's pastoral response to early industrial capitalism, in terms of papal leadership, can be characterized as both nostalgic and hostile. It rejected the new world being born, harkening back to Christendom and the traditional agrarian society that were fast disappearing. In addition, the centralization of the church, begun during the Counter-Reformation, intensified during this period. This trend led to a siege mentality, or "ghetto Catholicism." The enemy of the church was vaguely described as "modernism." The strategy, aspects of which continue today, climaxed with the *Syllabus of Errors* and the definition of papal infallibility at Vatican Council I. The loss of the Papal States was a major cause of the strategy's demise. The death of Pope Pius IX in 1878 signaled the end of its dominance.

This strategic response of rejection and siege mentality constituted the ecclesial context for ministry during the age of *laissez-faire* industrial capitalism (see Chart D, column I). Its central theme was the defense of tradition. Its modern enemy was liberalism—"free thought" in culture, democracy in politics, and a *laissez-faire* "free market" in the economic realm. The strategy was centered in Europe. Its intent was to preserve the cultural control of the church over society or, failing that, to retreat to a defensible fortress. The pursuit of this objective often involved an informal political alliance of the church hierarchy with the reactionary landed aristocracy of Europe—from whence much of the higher clergy came. The vehicle of the strategy was religious ministry to the life cycle (birth, growth, and death) through the local parish, organized around the sacramental system. The hierarchy of pastor, bishop, and pope presided directly and immediately over the strategy.

CHART D
THREE STRATEGIC PASTORAL RESPONSES

	I *Traditional Church* *(to 1878)*	*II* *Liberal Church* *(1878 to 1958)*	*III* *Prophetic Church* *(1958 to ?)*
Attitude	Reactionary	Adaptive	Transformative
Dominant	. . . Pius IX	Leo XIII-Pius XII	John XXIII . . .
Problematic	Faith and Tradition	Faith and Freedom	Faith and Justice
Form	Cultural Control	Political Interest Group	Cultural Vision
Alliance	Aristocracy	Middle Classes	Poor
Vehicle	Sacramental System	Parallel Structures	Basic Christian Community
Sector	Bishops and Pastors (Line)	Religious Professionals (Staff)	Laity (Constituency)
Geography	Europe	North America	Third World
Jesus	Christ the King (Defensive)	Christ the King (Offensive)	Servant Jesus
Spirituality	Legalistic/Devotional	Liturgical	Charismatic

The image of Jesus that prevailed during this period was that of "Christ the King," modeled after Israel's King David and the Roman emperors. However, this image assumed a defensive posture under siege from a hostile culture. The spirituality of the church's response was both legalistic and devotional.

In the ecclesial context of this pastoral strategy, the key tasks of the local parish were to protect the faithful, to conserve intact the deposit of faith, and to administer the sacraments. Church ministry, in turn, followed an authoritarian style. This strategy was more an expression of traditional Catholic culture than a model deliberately implemented. Although it may be rightly criticized, it did preserve many positive institutional and traditional values that were challenged by "modernization."

The church's well-ordered strategy went into crisis when liberal forces came together and overpowered the church's resistance. In economic terms, the church lost much of its secular privilege and extensive lands, including the Papal States of Italy. Politically, the liberal society broke the power of the European aristocracy and created new governments controlled by commercial and industrial elites. Thus, new social classes evolved—urban workers and an urban middle class—who were not part of the traditional Catholic strategy that had focused on the peasantry and the aristocracy. Culturally, liberalism marginalized Catholic intellectual life, which fell into a decadent scholasticism.

As a climax to the traditionalist strategy, Pope Pius IX condemned the proposition that "the Roman Pontiff can and should reconcile and harmonize himself with progress, with liberalism, and with recent civilization" (Proposition 80, *Syllabus of Errors*). However, after the death of Pius IX in 1878, his successor, Leo XIII, began a diplomatic outreach to liberalism (industrial capitalism) and modern civilization. That outreach marked a fundamentally different pastoral strategy for the Catholic Church in the twentieth century, and hence, a new ecclesial context for ministry. Occurring at precisely the time that the social welfare stage of capitalism was beginning to emerge, the new strategy opened new doors and provided the church with opportunities for a more creative role in the "modern world." Before turning to this new strategy, however, let us examine the new social context that made the strategy possible.

THE SECOND STAGE

The second stage of industrial capitalism, the social welfare form, and the related rise of a Catholic liberal strategy lasted roughly from the turn of the twentieth century until 1968. It was a more benevolent stage than its predecessor, in spite of the deep suffering that continued for many, and in spite of events such as the Great Depression of the 1930s. The benevolence of the period was not solely the result of agitation for reform, although pressure from reformers was a factor. Rather, the humanitarian thrust of the second stage was, in large part, a consequence of the historical/structural context that made such reform possible. Within the new context, reform was not only possible, but necessary in order to prevent gains by the secular Left. Thus, the church found an opening not present before. In order to understand the reasons for this opening, let us review the shifts in the second capitalistic stage.

Social Welfare Industrial Capitalism

The deep structures of this second stage, as in the first stage, remain capital and technology (see Chart C, column II). Their shape, however, had significantly altered. Capital was becoming national in its sphere of movement and influence; technology was moving into a capital/labor balance. Both of these shifts helped to make reform possible.

Capital became national as early competition yielded to virtual monopoly (or oligopoly) in basic industries. As a result, workers began to organize themselves into national labor unions. When they pressured industry for concessions in wages, working conditions, and benefits, the monopolistic national corporations were eventually able to make these concessions without fear of being undercut by maverick competitors. Of course, these concessions were not given easily, but by the middle of the twentieth century, Europe and Western North America had achieved a firm management/labor alliance. In the automobile industry, for example, a few large car companies dominated the industry and accepted, in principle, autoworkers' unions.

Likewise, as *technology* moved into a capital/labor balance, there were more goods over which to bargain. Increased productivity, due to technological advance, was laying the foundation for a consumer society. In the automobile industry, Henry Ford produced a car that even his own workers could buy—a phenomenon unheard of before that time.

Economically, therefore, the industrial working class eventually found itself in a favorable situation—demand for labor and productivity were both increasing. The framework of less competitive national corporations was paralleled by national labor organizations. Where exploitation had been the dominant theme of the earlier period, prosperity now became the basic trend— even though not all shared in it.

Politically, the national consolidation of capital required a state system that could facilitate that structure on a national scale. That meant the emergence of a national regulatory state, involved in interstate commerce, the national banking system, the stock market, etc. The new regulatory state, willing to intervene in a moderate fashion in the "free market," was also pressured by workers' movements and other social welfare lobbies to enact the progressive social welfare legislation we know today—social security, minimum wage, unemployment compensation, collective bargaining rights, etc. Where Adam Smith had been the key theorist for *laissez-faire* industrial capitalism, Lord Maynard Keynes played that role for the social welfare stage. During this period, the state was explicitly concerning itself with the "common good."

Culturally, freedom ceased to connote solely negative license. Instead, it came to signify positive opportunity for large sectors of the public. This sense of opportunity reached its highest point in the civil rights movement of the 1960s and the "dream" of Dr. Martin Luther King, Jr. We call this new stage "social liberalism," in contrast to the libertarianism of the preceding stage.

During the second stage of industrial capitalism, the social system set itself in strong opposition to the new communist states. These states were rapidly consolidating their power—beginning with the Russian Revolution early in the twentieth century and broadening with the annexation of Eastern European states after World War II. Proposing many of the same social welfare themes, these states began a rapid, if late, industrialization based on the model of Western technology. Their political life, however, was marked at best by authoritarianism and at worst by repression, both of which were rooted in the monopoly of power vested in the state under the dominance of a single party. In these states, practitioners of religion, including Roman Catholics, were harassed and even persecuted. As a result, Catholicism rallied to

Western capitalism as the defender of democratic freedom and of respect for religion. Thus, the onslaught of the Cold War marked the church as well as the greater society.

Let us now examine in more detail the church's pastoral response to social welfare industrial capitalism.

Pastoral Response: The Liberal Strategy

Where the earlier church strategy had been reactionary, the new pastoral strategy was adaptive—although at times schizophrenic. The church looked to social welfare liberalism as a missionary terrain it could enter and, it was hoped, restore in Christ. At the same time, the church tried to protect its own internal life from "contamination" by the liberal spirit. Defending democracy against communist states, the church struggled within itself against initiatives for democracy, due process, and decentralization, among countless other emerging trends.

The liberal strategy began with Leo XIII, a leader who, while still a traditionalist, had switched from hostile rejection to diplomatic outreach toward the modern world. The strategy continued throughout the twentieth century, despite struggles and setbacks. It climaxed in Cold War Catholicism under Pope Pius XII (see p. 71, Chart D, column II).

The key theme of the liberal strategy was the adaptation of the traditional religious institution to an environment of change—to liberal economic, political, and cultural life under social welfare capitalism. This process can be described as the engagement of faith with freedom, or liberalization. Economically, the papacy shifted from a foundation in agriculture (the Papal States) to an extensive stock market portfolio. Politically, it came to terms with liberal governments—because they were not going to disappear—eventually legitimizing in Europe and Latin America the concept of "Christian Democracy." Finally, with the groundbreaking work of the American Jesuit theologian, John Courtney Murray, the church accepted the full range of secular democracy. Culturally, Catholicism began a revival of Thomism—eventually in dialogue with modern philosophy—thereby offering a more socially-oriented definition of the "common good" as a counterbalance to individualistic liberalism.

Unlike the earlier strategy, the new pastoral strategy did not center on cultural control. Rather, it focused on a many-pronged influence model, organized through "parallel Catholic structures" (schools, hospitals, political parties, Catholic Action organizations, etc.) that intervened at strategic points in the new social complex. The liberal strategy of the church thus created explicitly Catholic versions of modern social institutions and movements. Catholic education, of course, played the central role in this strategic model.

Initiation of the new strategy was increasingly transferred from the traditional church hierarchy to specialized religious professionals—chaplains, teachers, hyphenated-priests, religious, and even a limited number of the laity. The hierarchy was responsible for overseeing the strategy, rather than initiating it on the local level. This division of responsibility paralleled the separation of ownership and management in the social welfare stage of industrial capitalism—a division that replaced the absolute control of the independent entrepreneur in the *laissez-faire* stage. Control was now mediated and indirect.

As the liberal strategy evolved, church offices were operated in a manner that increasingly resembled the functioning of a corporation. They acquired specialized branches, increased their operating budgets, and greatly expanded their bureaucracies. At the parish level, the pastor became administrator of a large "plant," not unlike a middle-level executive with significant financial and personnel responsibilities.

The geographic center of the new strategy shifted from Europe to North America. The North American church was not a leading theological center that offered deep intellectual insights. Rather, it served as a pragmatic model for the new church. It was founded on the principle of separation of church and state and was thoroughly immersed in the liberal world. For these reasons, the influence of the North American church on global Catholicism increased considerably.

The religious symbolism of the social welfare stage continued to center on "Christ the King," reaching back to the main lines of Constantinean Christianity. However, the church was no longer on the defensive. Instead, its posture shifted to a missionary offensive; its objective was to conquer liberalism for the church. Gradually, the individualistic, internalized, subjective piety of the devotions gave way to a more corporate, external, objective, and liturgical style of spirituality, thus reflecting the church's re-newed sense of organic community. Gustavo Gutiérrez has de-scribed this shift as a neo-Constantinean strategy.

The gains of the liberal strategy, won throughout the twentieth century, were finally consolidated in Vatican Council II. While the achievements of the Council appear to be the gains of a more contemporary generation, they are actually the fruit of struggles that began at the end of the nineteenth century. Their consolida-tion, rather than strengthening the liberal strategy, offered a springboard for a new pastoral strategy.

One major struggle carried out over the last one hundred years became the central feature of the presently emerging pastoral strategy. That feature is the *social thrust* of modern Catholicism. Its role is necessarily heightened in the context of the third stage of industrial capitalism—the stage we are currently entering.

THE THIRD STAGE

The third historical/structural stage of industrialization in the context of Western capitalism and of church strategic response is only beginning to take shape. It is important to note that this is indeed a new and different social stage, one that will not be as benevolent as the one preceding it, nor carry within itself the hope of the future that lessened the hardship of *laissez-faire* industrial capitalism. In every area of life—economic, political, and cultural—we are moving into a grimmer future. The daily papers and evening news express these facts with all their national and international implications. We do not wish to be unduly pessimis-tic. Pessimism is not a great motivator for social change. How-ever, if we are to meet the challenge of this new age, we must face squarely and realistically the full range of problems it presents. These are profound problems, calling us to shape a pastoral re-sponse equal to the societal crisis they have created. Let us look first at the shape of that crisis.

National Security Industrial Capitalism

Again, the two deep structures in this third stage of industrial capitalism are the structures of *capital* and *technology*. Both structures are undergoing fundamental change (see p. 66, Chart

C, column III). Capital is becoming increasingly *transnational* and technology is becoming more *capital-intensive* (using less labor in relation to capital). These two shifts have laid the foundation for a third stage of world industrialization, beyond which lies a new form of society. We call this third phase "national security industrial capitalism," taking its name from the new form of the state.

The first change—the development of *transnational capital*—is evident even in something as common as advertisements in business magazines. The dominant feature of our economic life is now the transnational corporation and the transnational bank. A recent ad for a Wall Street investment firm portrayed its communications room, filled with desks and telephones, where daily decisions are made concerning the movement of capital. The communications room was set against the background of a huge satellite photo of the earth. Beneath was the caption: "The room is now global." The ad implies that the networks and criteria for movement of capital are no longer national, but are now transnational in breadth, with implications worldwide. What is the social impact of this shift?

The impact is brutal. The internationalization of capital has destroyed one of the features that made social welfare capitalism a relatively benevolent phase. That is, it has upset the national balance of power between capital and labor, allowing transnational capital to increase its control over national economies. It does this two ways.

First, it ends the monopolistic conditions that made it possible for corporations to bend before workers' demands without being undercut by competitors. Now, the formerly unchallenged industrial economy of North America is competing with advanced industrial bases in Europe and Japan, the Third World, and the communist states.

Second, global capital will flow wherever the return is greatest. Returns will be greatest where wages are restrained and taxes low (hence, where social services are curtailed). This development places authoritarian states that repress their workers and provide few social services at a competitive advantage in the world market. Hence, the flourishing of dictatorships and the crisis of democracy worldwide.

This movement is restoring *laissez-faire* competition on a global scale, with the same "punishments" for benevolence and "rewards" for ruthlessness. However, the rewards and punishments are now meted out to nations rather than to family firms. Thus, in the third stage of industrial capitalism, transnational capital outflanks national workers' movements. When workers in one country, or one region of a given country, develop a strong labor movement, capital simply moves elsewhere. This development has led to North/South tensions both domestically and internationally—domestically between the sunbelt and snowbelt states, and internationally between First World and Third World countries. These new tensions complement East/West tensions that predominated in the period of social welfare capitalism.

As detente between the East and West deteriorates, these tensions are again returning to the fore. However, the tensions are no longer predominantly political—as they were during the Cold War era. Increasingly, they are economic tensions, as East and West compete within the world market system, particularly over access to strategic resources.

Transnational capital not only outflanks workers by geographic diversification, but also by industrial diversification. We are now in the age of the global conglomerate, not the single industry corporation. Today, a business enterprise may own a car rental agency, a bread company, extensive real estate holdings, a steel company, and energy interests. As a result, the conglomerate can subsidize the losses from a labor strike in one industry with the profits of its other holdings. Thus, labor is doubly vulnerable in the new period. Moreover, since global conglomerates dominate the major media (television, radio, newspapers, magazines), it is hard for labor to get a fair public hearing.

Capital is not the only aspect of industrialization that has been transformed in the new stage. *Technology* has become increasingly capital-intensive, using more machinery, computers, and energy. In the preceding period, the capital/labor balance provided abundant production along with the capacity to absorb most of society's labor supply—except during periods of cyclical downturn. Now, however, people speak of "structural unemployment" or permanent "marginalization" from the main economy. In the Third World, such marginalization means that the masses of the peasantry, every day displaced from the agricultural sector, go to cities that do not need their labor.

In the First World, this phenomenon means plant closings and capital flight. Cities that were once hungry for labor are marginalizing minorities, especially the young and the elderly. We are witnessing the creation of a permanent underclass in the so-called "developed" world, a class that will never enter the mainstream of productive life in contemporary society.

There are, of course, solutions to the problem of human marginalization. The changes required to humanize the new world are theoretically simple. For example, industrial technology could be reoriented to serve basic human needs. The work week could be shortened so that work could be more equitably distributed. The labor-intensive service sector could be expanded. However, these solutions are not feasible within the unregulated competitive transnational structure of the current stage of industrial capitalism.

Such changes in the economic structures of society would severely weaken the international competitive posture of the nation that implements them. First, the nation would be competing against states that do not serve basic needs, maintain shorter work weeks, or have expanded service sectors. Consequently, these other nations would be more attractive environments for investment capital since their wages and taxes would be lower and returns on investments would be greater. Second, any nation that moves to full employment finds its labor force more militant. Workers are not afraid of being fired for their activities since there are other jobs available. Lack of control over the labor market is thus another quality that undermines the attractiveness of such a society to investment capital. (The only exceptions to this trend are the communist systems that maintain full employment. In these countries, however, the state is both repressive and has a monopoly on jobs. Dissidents often find themselves without jobs, or with the most menial ones.)

The structural changes in the deep structures of capital and technology will have obvious consequences in the functional regions.

Economic life in this new period will be different from what it was in the period we are leaving. First, it will be marked by the serious problem of structural unemployment or marginalization. Second, the management/labor alliance in effect since World War II has begun to disintegrate. New class conflicts will be felt across the society. Third, the trend of upward mobility will shift to one of downward mobility for the majority of the population. Central to this third shift is a condition of permanent inflation rooted in increased military spending, the high cost of present technologies in basic needs areas (e.g., food, medicine, housing, and health care), the oligopolistic price-fixing of multinational corporations, and the restraints on the growth of the public service sector. Even among the middle class, the ingredients of the "American Dream" are slipping from the people's grasp. One's own home, a new car, and college for the children are beyond the reach of many in the new generation who once took these things for granted. People are nervous—and rightly so. Their economic future is not promising.

It is in the *political* system, however, that one sees some of the most frightening changes; it is this system that is the source of the period's name—"national security" industrial capitalism. Social welfare considerations have yielded to national security imperatives, just as *laissez-faire* behavior once gave way to social welfare objectives. The domain of national security has expanded to include cultural, political, and economic as well as military dimensions—in both domestic and foreign policies. The state has become to the world market what the corporation once was to the national market, and before that, the family firm to the local market. The state is now charged, not only with moderate economic regulation within the boundaries of the national economy, but with streamlining the whole national system for efficient transnational competition.

This domestic "streamlining" for reasons of international competition entails three key political actions: (1) the restraint of wages; (2) the curtailment of social services; and (3) the increase in governmental authority to use coercive methods to achieve its goals. Although, in the extreme, this turn-of-events could culminate in dictatorship, the political shift can also take moderate forms.

We are experiencing a moderate variation of this trend in the current U.S. political scene. Generally speaking, the drift in

American politics is away from grassroots participation and accountability toward a more technocratic elitism. However, a currently respectable "neo-conservatism" can easily become a right-
wing reformulation of the American political purpose. (For
political interpretation along these lines, see Michael Crozier, Sa-
muel P. Huntington, Joji Watanuki, *The Crisis of Democracy:
Report on the Governability of Democracies to the Trilateral
Commission*, New York: New York University Press, 1975.)

Preoccupation with national security is also evident in the contemporary *cultural* system. The earlier focus on the promises of
the future—never-ending progress and greater and greater
abundance—has recently shifted to such themes as "the new austerity," "lowered expectations," and "discipline." The definition of freedom, having once changed from "license" to "opportunity," now centers on the theme of "security"—but security
for the few and security to preserve profitable investments. Political and civil freedoms are dramatically weakened according to
this new definition.

The New Right, which is attempting to gain political control in
this new situation, has pursued a devious strategy. Rather than
focus on the deep structural causes of people's anxiety, it is catering to their fears. It promises to provide law and order, to de-
fend the family, to restore the "American Dream." However, in
actuality, this New Right is a vicious force ultimately undermin-
ing all of these values.

By catering to fear, the New Right hopes to drive a strategic
wedge between the middle class on one side, and labor unions and
the poor on the other. Labor unions and the poor are being used
as scapegoats for the social problems that are threatening the security of the middle class.

The only creative response to this crisis, however, will be a new
and broad coalition of the middle class, labor unions, and the
poor, in cooperation with community institutions like the church.
Only such a coalition can challenge the structural roots of the
problem and work to build a new society.

The obsession with national security has had profound effects
on industrial communist as well as capitalist countries. As communist countries are integrated into the world market system,
they and the capitalist national security states appear to be con-

verging in negative ways. This trend may culminate in a synthesis of the worst features of capitalism and the worst features of communism. Those who frame the question as a choice between big government or big business—alternately industrial communism or industrial capitalism—miss the point entirely. The answer is not more centralization in public or private forms, but community control over capital and technology.

While the new stage of industrial capitalism will be difficult for our own society, especially for those already "marginalized," it will be disastrous for the Third World. In the Third World there is no social welfare base to cushion the impact of the national security state.

The experience of the Third World will be pivotal for church and society in the third stage of industrialization. Walbert Bühlmann has estimated in his book *The Coming of the Third Church* (Maryknoll, N.Y.: Orbis Books, 1977) that by the year 2000, a full 70 percent of the world's Catholics will live in the Third World, 48 percent of them in Latin America. The Third World, Bühlmann argues, represents a new and dynamic "church of the South," pointing the way into the third millennium, much as the "Church of the West" carved the way through the second millennium and the "Church of the East" laid the foundation in the first millennium. Bühlmann's observation brings us directly to the question of church pastoral strategy in the period we are now entering.

Pastoral Response: The Radical Strategy

What is the pastoral style appropriate to a society entering into the third stage of industrialization, characterized as "national security industrial capitalism"? The style needs to be *transformative* (see p. 71, Chart D, column III). It looks forward to a new society and a new church beyond the boundaries of either industrial capitalist or industrial communist forms found in the period of late industrialization.

In the contemporary Catholic community, there are two major interpretations of this transformative posture. One appeals to a humanistic socialist tradition; the other searches out a new utopian vision that builds upon the "Third Way" teaching of modern Catholic social thought. Underlying both perspectives is a central principle for humanizing the new stage. This principle, the transformation of capital and technology to serve basic human needs and fundamental human rights, is accountable to community at every level, from the local to the global.

If the social style of the pastoral response is transformative, the faith problematic in which it is grounded is *justice*. Justice, in this case, is set over and against the dominant theme of national security. The transformative style, grounded in justice, contrasts sharply with the earlier adaptive style of the liberal church, a response that was organized under the faith problematic of freedom. Likewise, it contrasts with the early reactionary strategy organized under the problematic of tradition. In this new style, justice is no longer a subdivision of moral theology, but a reconstituting vision for faith and theology. Because this new strategy digs to the root of the problem, it can be called a "radical" strategy.

With Pope John XXIII the radical strategy began to take shape, although at that time it was no more than a diplomatic opening to the Left (recalling Pope Leo XIII's diplomatic opening to liberalism). Vatican Council II served as a springboard for the new strategy. However, it is in the church of the South—in the Third World—that its main lines are beginning to emerge. Even at this early stage, it may be helpful to suggest some of the lines this pastoral strategy will be taking.

The form of the strategy focuses on *cultural vision*. This vision, derived from dialogue within the church as well as outside, seeks a new and more just society. This vision will inform both social and ecclesial praxis. The approach of this "utopian" vision contrasts markedly with the self-interest model so prevalent in the liberal strategy and with the cultural control that characterized the traditionalist strategy.

The major social linkage of the church in the radical strategy is with the poor. The association with the underclass contrasts sharply with the focus on the middle class in the social welfare stage and the identification with the aristocracy during the age of *laissez-faire* industrial capitalism. The initiating sector of the radical strategy is the laity—rather than the specialized religious professionals or the church hierarchy who initiated the earlier strategies. The geographic center of the radical response to capitalism is, as mentioned earlier, the Third World—particularly the heavily-populated countries of Latin America.

The vehicle of the strategy, the "basic Christian community" (*comunidad de base*), has grown beyond the specialized Catholic Action movements of the liberal stage and the parishes of the traditionalist stage. The symbolic interpretation has shifted from the Davidic image of "Christ the King," dominant since Constantinean Christianity, to a mosaic image of a "Prophetic Servant Jesus." In turn, the spirituality that characterizes the new pastoral response is more "charismatic," that is, spontaneous, small group-oriented, and biblical.

In this strategy, we are entering not simply a new response to industrialization, but a whole new form of the church—one that is altering elements that have dominated the church since the time of Constantine and perhaps ever since the apostle Paul and the rise of the Greek Church. The radical strategy, therefore, is not merely a short-term traditional strategy. Rather, it is a profound shift that terminates Constantinean Christianity, retrieving neglected elements of the pre-Constantinean and perhaps pre-Pauline forms.

While the radical strategy is centered in the activities of small grassroots groups that constitute the basic Christian community, there is also a significant *transnational character* to the strategy. The church is a genuine transnational actor, one that is present and active across national boundaries. Thus, there is a paradoxical two-way thrust to the strategy, the first toward the grassroots and the second toward the transnational arena. Thus, within the new strategy, there is a combination of decentralization and broad networking.

Since transnationalism is a special characteristic of the new period, it will become a special characteristic of the church's new strategy. The events that transpire anywhere within the global church are of immediate interest to the local churches throughout the world. As local churches become more involved in the actions of the transnational church, that church will move further and further from the direct control of the Roman Curia and increasingly develop transnational linkages among regional and national episcopal conferences and joint pastoral councils of priests, religious, and especially laity, accountable to networks of basic Christian communities.

Pastoral strategy during this third stage of industrial capitalism is, of course, strongly influenced by the central theme of justice, i.e., the transformation of society. For example, the task of ministry today is not to protect the faithful from the challenge to tradition, nor to help them adapt to liberal change, but to offer spiritual resources and social tools for the transformation of society along lines that promote justice and respect human values. This task is part of the effort of building the Reign of God.

Of profound importance for the new strategy has been the social theology enunciated in the Second Vatican Council and in the Synods of 1971 and 1975, as well as the social teaching of Pope John XXIII and later, Pope Paul VI, especially in *Populorum Progressio* (1967) and *Octogesima Adveniens* (1971). The particular social teaching of Pope John Paul II, especially as enunciated during his visits to numerous countries of varied conditions, will, of course, be immensely influential. It is still too early to discern fully the direction of that teaching, but it appears to offer elements of a radical social analysis, an ambiguous general social strategy, and a conservative religious style. How that will manifest itself in the life of the church remains to be seen.

In the midst of these many influences, one very significant theological position is determinative in the radical strategy. This position sees the process of *evangelization*—the spreading of the "Good News"—as mediated through the poor and oppressed. Power and wealth are no longer perceived as supportive of evangelization. The significant witness of the contemporary Latin American church, for instance, has been its gradual effort to divorce evangelization from the dominant power structures and to trust the resources of ordinary people. This move constitutes a profound shift in the perspective of the church, one with significant historic consequences. In fact, it marks the end of Constantinean Christianity. It is a shift that demands a price, however, one that is now being paid with the blood of martyrs.

SUMMARY/CONCLUSION

In this chapter, we have attempted to illustrate the ways in which social analysis can help us to understand the context of the pastoral ministries of the church. Using as our major example the process of industrialization in Western capitalist form, we have traced three historical stages. Each of these stages has called forth a particular style of pastoral response:

- *Laissez-faire industrial capitalism* **called forth the** *traditionalist* **strategy.**
- *Social welfare industrial capitalism* **called forth the** *liberal* **strategy.**
- *National security industrial capitalism* **is now calling forth the** *radical* **strategy.**

What lessons can we learn from this particular illustration of social analysis as a tool of pastoral practice?

First, we need to recall that the historical periods described in this text are abstractions. As such, they attempt to condense complex data into manageable forms. These forms are helpful, not because they offer precise representations of the historical periods, but because, by simplifying the processes, they can stimulate a greater understanding of the periods. As we emphasized in Chapter 1, social analysis never provides the *complete* picture. However, it does offer a set of important questions that help to expose the basic contours of the reality before us.

Second, we can appreciate that historical/structural analysis is important precisely *because* it situates specific circumstances in a general framework. The behavior of individuals—business leaders, workers, government officials, church leaders—is regarded not only in the private personal context; it is examined as action conditioned by a specific social context. We understand the significance of structures—economic, political, cultural—and note that as the structures change, the responses of individuals must also be transformed.

Third, the understanding of historical change frees us from "feeling guilty" about past responses and prevents us from being overly critical in regard to decisions made by earlier generations. Pastoral responses appropriate to the period of *laissez-faire* industrial capitalism are not appropriate in the present period of national security industrial capitalism. However, this fact does not imply that those strategies were ill-conceived or out-of-place in their own particular time. There were strengths as well as weaknesses in earlier responses. We need to learn from both and seek the best responses for today.

Fourth, through the application of social analysis, we can also come to a better understanding of both the commonness and the uniqueness of our own national experience. The church experience in the United States, for example, and we refer in particular to the Catholic experience, is both like and unlike the experiences of the global church. It would be a mistake to argue that the crisis that we face in this country is so similar to that experienced by the rest of the world that we need not reflect upon our own uniqueness. However, it would be equally mistaken to argue that we are so different that we have nothing to learn from—or give to—the international church. This lesson is important to recall in this third stage of industrial capitalism, particularly as we study the experiences of the Third World. The church of the United States can learn much, for example, from the Latin American church and its strategy of basic Christian communities.

Conclusion

Effective pastoral action—the linking of faith and justice—requires adequate social knowledge. This thesis is the premise of our study. In order to respond effectively to situations of injustice in today's world, and to people's related spiritual hunger, we must strive to understand the social reality in all its complexity. Evangelization and ministry that include action on behalf of justice need to be "contextualized." The creation of such a framework is the task of the social analysis we have described.

We repeat once again: social analysis is not the *answer* to social problems, but a *tool* for dealing with them. We have offered a general explanation of social analysis and provided examples of its function as a tool for understanding the dynamics of change, development, and industrialization. The use of social analysis in each of these cases has suggested specific pastoral responses. Surely, the reader will think of other implications of and applications for social analysis, as well as other pastoral responses. This, at least, is our hope.

LIMITS OF ANALYSIS

Since social analysis is only one part of the struggle to link faith and justice, we conclude with a few words about its limits.

Social analysis has three interrelated and serious limitations that stem from its roots in the "rationalism" of the Enlightenment: (1) it is only a *negative* instrument; (2) it moves only in the *scientific* thought mode; and (3) it uses *elite* language. These limitations should not preclude the use of social analysis. However, it is important that the analysis be corrected by resources that go beyond Enlightenment rationality—namely, by the creative power of *culture*. Before discussing culture, however, let us review the three limitations.

89

First, social analysis is only a *negative* instrument. By that we mean it has the destructive power to tear away the mystification of our social world and to unveil the deep structures that control it. Our response to that disclosure is often a feeling of powerlessness. We are overwhelmed and immobilized. (We experience the "paralysis of analysis.") What can we do to challenge such powerful structures? Equally critical, what would be a creative alternative?

To move beyond this feeling of powerlessness, we need the creative resources of *vision* and *energy*. The condemnation of unjust structures is not enough. We need something that calls us to a different future, something that draws us in a positive direction. In addition, we need a source of energy, of courage, and of dedication. As Christians, we look to our spiritual resources for vision and energy. In more secular terms, we might say we look to culture.

Culture is the medium through which the spiritual visions and energies of a society are expressed. This vision and its energies can take many forms, but we believe its source is spiritual. The rise of the modern world, despite its negative scientific rationality, was initially energized by the quasi-religious vision of progress and freedom. Our point is not to argue for one particular vision, but to emphasize the need for a positive cultural vision that energizes people and empowers them.

Second, social analysis is a *scientific* effort; that is, it uses analytical tools to divide reality into separate and abstract parts. The social analyst is like the medical pathologist who looks at parts of the body in isolation in order to diagnose illness and prescribe treatment. However, if the analysis breaks a living body into its component parts, it risks destroying its creative life. If a social analyst takes away life, what will return it—at least in social terms?

That task falls to the *artist*—not only the artist of high culture (the great painters, composers, and authors of classical literature), but artists whose roots are found in popular culture. We believe that the artistic impulse is the creative force in modern civilization. It is the spiritual source from which vision and energy flow. While we need to analyze society with scientific rigor, we must be wary of destroying that impulse.

Social analysis will not reveal the artistic creativity of ordinary people as they shape their family lives, their communities, and ultimately, the whole world. The social analyst knows only scientific instruments. Thus, a new society built only on "rationalist" resources, will inevitably be centered on a "scientific state." This state tends to crush the rooted community and to destroy the artistic creativity of ordinary people.

Third, the language of technical social analysis is *elitist*. Locked in the chains of a technical language, it has little communicative power. (We confess to a fault perhaps all too obvious in this study: frequent use of technical language which, while precise, may hinder communication.) The alternative to this technical language is the *symbolic dimension of popular culture*. Thus, we emphasize the need to explore the symbolism, myths, dreams, and visions of ordinary people. For example, a purely economic analysis of the situation of blacks or Hispanics in the United States would overlook areas of great significance to the reality they experience—e.g., religion, family heritage, music, etc.

Another way of expressing the importance of attention to popular culture is to return to the "pastoral circle" described in Chapter 1. The "experience" we speak of as the primary data for the process of the pastoral circle is not, of course, "raw" experience. What we come into contact with is always mediated, interpreted, received. Hence we must not think of experience as isolated or unrelated, existing in some kind of vacuum. At each point of the pastoral circle, we are in touch with this primary data. But, and this is an important second point to emphasize about experience, neither is it simply the "empirical." Rather it also must include the "experiential." The empirical refers mainly to the factual data, to that which can be measured quantitatively. The experiential takes into account the total human person, the lived encounter with reality which involves mind and body, senses and heart. The myths and visions of people, grounded in the experiential, are indicative of their beliefs and values at the deepest level.

Again, it is not simply the data, the facts used in the analysis, that reflect a people's culture and values. Equally important is the *communication* of the social situation, the artistic expression through which the experience is conveyed to other people. Stories, art, song, poetry, dance—all can communicate in ways that are far more insightful than the scientific words of rational analysis. In fact, the struggles of ordinary people are frequently presented in art forms long before any "sophisticated" analysis is offered. The spirituals of black slaves in the American South portrayed the conditions of slavery and the hopes of freedom in compelling fashion long before they were written into textbooks and novels. Today, "street theater" in the cities of many Third World countries communicates a strong social message. In 1975, the Center of Concern collaborated on the powerful Appalachian pastoral letter "This Land is Home to Me." The pastoral came alive when its original prose draft was translated into a poetic rendering mindful of the songs of the Appalachian culture.

We stress the importance of culture because many people committed to social justice have tended to ignore it. Both liberals and radicals often construct and communicate analyses and strategies based solely on "rationality"—but a rationality that is insensitive to the role of symbols in everyday experience. The failure to grasp the creative role of rooted, passion-filled, meta-rational, collective symbols can be disastrous, countering the effectiveness of social change strategies.

An illustration of such a failure can be found in the attitude of progressive social forces toward the highly emotional triad of "flag, family, and faith." These symbols are expressions of three basic social institutions central to the culture of ordinary people: *nation* (flag); *kinship*, including neighborhood (family); and *religion* (faith). They are also expressions that, by and large, have been captured by the forces of the Right in the United States. Frequently, they are used in political campaigns that stand in opposition to the quest for social justice. By failing to take seriously the power of these symbols, liberal and radical social forces have lost effectiveness. (For further discussion of this point, see Joe Holland, *Flag, Faith and Family: Rooting the American Left in Everyday Symbols*, Chicago: New Patriotic Alliance, 1979.) We need to regain deeply-rooted symbols for the cause of social justice action, and good social analysis will help to meet this need.

THEOLOGY AND ANALYSIS

We want to emphasize once again the relationship between theological reflection and social analysis. Though they have been described as two distinct moments in the "pastoral circle," it should now be clear that they are interdependent. In social analysis for pastoral action, the link between faith and justice requires that the theological reflection grow out of the analysis.

To be frank, the theological reflection we need is difficult to find in North America. Or perhaps it is more correct to say that theologians who are reflecting in this way are not yet numerous or prominent. Most theologians who are concerned with social justice practice theological methods that do not begin with social analysis. Thus, the contemporary North American theological community is confronted by two major tasks: (1) to forge a strong link between theology and social science; and (2) to link the theological process with the experience of the poor and oppressed.

Today, many efforts are being made to promote theological reflection that is sensitive to these two tasks. Social scientists, theologians, and people involved in social struggles are coming together to discuss various problems and strategic responses. Dialogues between First and Third World theologians, and among black, Hispanic, Native American, and feminist groups are taking place. It will become increasingly important for seminaries and theological centers in North America to respond to this call for deeper theological reflection. While the reflective work stimulated by the Medellín (1968) and Puebla (1979) conferences of the Latin American church continues to be highly influential, it is neither desirable nor possible to simply "import" the process (or product) to our particular cultural environment.

WHERE NEXT?

"Where do we go from here?" This question may come to our readers as they search for ways to apply social analysis to concrete efforts for social justice action. For those who want to apply the pastoral tool of social analysis on the local level, or to focus their efforts on a particular problem, we suggest the following:

1. **Gather together a team of people who have varied experiences and academic backgrounds—especially in the social sciences—to assist in the task of analysis.**

2. **Answer a simple questionnaire in order to construct a "context" for your local reality. (See sample on pp. 106-9.)**
3. **Evaluate some of the current efforts to meet the justice situations facing your area. (See pp. 110-12 for suggested criteria for evaluation.)**
4. **Identify the key structures that influence the present situation.**
5. **Discuss the relevancy of the different models of analysis presented in this study (change, development, industrialization) to your situation.**
6. **Test some suggested pastoral responses in light of your analysis.**
7. **Probe the theological issues that arise in the course of your efforts.**

Using the tool of social analysis, people who act on behalf of justice will gain clearer insight into the complexities of the situations confronting them and will design more effective strategies in response. The linking of faith and justice in the social struggles of our times requires such clear insight and effective strategies in order to succeed.

Our final word is a plea for patience and persistence. Social analysis is an art that is developed gradually over a period of many years. There is no "instant coffee" version of social analysis. It requires deepening oneself in the experience of injustice, in the theological resources, and in the disciplines of social science. To be most effective, it should engage whole communities—people working together—rather than isolated individuals. Finally, we urge that analysis be pursued in a framework of prayer, for ultimately it is the Spirit of the Servant Jesus who reveals to us the "signs of the times."

Afterword

Social Analysis:
A Practical Methodology

by Peter Henriot, S.J.

"But how does one *do* social analysis?"

This practical question has been repeatedly put to the staff of the Center of Concern in recent years—both by people with whom we work and by ourselves. The "how to" question comes up strongly as people become convinced of the importance of a deeper look at our social reality and want to put into practice the tool for opening up that reality.

When we wrote the first edition of *Social Analysis: Linking Faith and Justice* in 1980, we specifically avoided offering a simple "one-two-three" approach to the task. The booklet was not conceived as a "manual" for easy operation of a new social technology. Rather, we felt it would first of all be helpful to explain the background and theory of the social analytical method and then to give some detailed examples of its use in understanding change, development, and industrialization. Some general hints at practical methodology were, of course, contained in what we wrote, but no full-scale plan was offered.

Over the past two years, all of our staff have developed further approaches to the task of social analysis. In a variety of

95

workshops across the United States and Canada and in several countries of Europe, Africa, Latin America, and Asia, we have made the methodological steps of social analysis more explicit and practical. This refinement has deepened our own understanding of both the potential and the limits of the analytical approach.

In what follows, we offer the outline of one particular practical methodology. We emphasize that it is one among many possible outlines and that its elements are not totally original with us. But it is an approach which many who have made our workshops have found helpful. The elements of the approach are grouped under four headings: (1) conversion, (2) description, (3) analysis, and (4) conclusions.

I. Conversion

The first step in doing social analysis is to make explicit the values which we bring to the task. That is, we need to be in touch with the perspectives, biases, stances which influence the questioning we do and the judgments we make. As we have emphasized repeatedly, no social analysis is "value free."

We do this by questioning ourselves about fundamentals. What are our basic beliefs and primary values? What are the foundations for our different actions? What has the most effect on the positions we take on various issues? These and similar questions begin to uncover the stance from which we do social analysis.

We need also to formulate the dimensions of the scripture and of the church's social teaching which influence our analysis. For example, the sacredness of the human person and the consequent respect for human dignity means that a primary question we will always ask in any situation is, "What is happening to people?" In particular, we will ask, "What is happening to the poor?" This is true because the "option for the poor" is fundamental to the Christian perspective and response to social reality. In one sense, we can say that the poor offer a "privileged hermeneutic" or primary point of interpretation in our understanding of the world today.

The first step in a practical methodology for social analysis is called "conversion" because it implies a turning to values. It serves as a way of opening us up to the more important elements of the situation we are understanding, by putting them in a context of the fundamentals which guide us. Done in a group, this step in the exercise also clarifies the commonalities and differences which will be influencing the subsequent discussion.

II. Description

The next step to take in social analysis is simply to make a general description of the situation we are trying to understand. We may be studying (1) a social problem (e.g., unemployment, inadequate housing, lack of agricultural development, etc.); (2) an institution (e.g., school, parish, corporation, etc.); or (3) a geographical entity (e.g., neighborhood, village, region, nation, etc.). We may take an *impressionistic* approach to the task of description. We gather facts and trends by way of brainstorming, telling stories, getting in touch with people's experiences. What is happening in this particular situation? What would a few photographs of the situation reveal? How would we talk about a few of the most prominent features of this situation?

Or we may choose a more *systematic* approach. In a very orderly fashion we gather all the pertinent information about the situation. We could use a questionnaire (e.g., see the form on pages 106-9) in order to probe the various sectors of our social reality. What are the important categories? What are the elements which help us best describe the situation?

Whatever approach we take—or mix of approaches—the important thing to remember is that we are primarily *describing*. We are not yet going into any deeper study of the particular situation, nor attempting to understand its relationship to the larger, more general social situation. We are not making any evaluation or reaching any conclusions in the sense of doing an explicit, formal analysis.

This step of description is to help us enter into the picture, get in touch with the experience of the situation, and begin also to point out the more important elements. We may also in this step of description make more explicit what it is in the situation which first drew us to study the situation—e.g., people are hurting, the pace of change is extremely rapid, some people are prospering more than others, we no longer have control over our local decisions, etc.

III. Analysis

Having made our brief description of the situation, we now move to the more formal analysis. We have defined social analysis as "the effort to obtain a more complete picture of a social situation by exploring its historical and structural relationships." We can go about that task by working through a series of four questions about the history, structures, values, and direction of the situation we are analyzing.

A. What is the main line of *history* of this situation?
We look at a situation with the eyes of historical consciousness and begin to perceive the deep background influences of the past on the present.

1. What have been the major stages (periods) through which this situation has moved?
2. What dynamic patterns of development can be observed?
3. What have been key turning points in the development of the situation?
4. Can we name major events which have influenced the course of the history of this situation? E.g., national events, government actions, church decisions, etc.

B. What are the major *structures* which influence this situation?
Structures shape the situation in a variety of ways. They are the institutions, processes, and patterns which are determining factors in the outcome of social reality. Some structures are obvious; others are hidden; all are interrelated. We suggest here four ways in which society is organized and list some structures to which we should pay attention.

1. What are the major *economic* structures which determine how society organizes *resources*? E.g.:
   —production, distribution, exchange, consumption
   —capital, labor, technology

  —concentrations, conglomerates
  —tax policies, interest rates
2. What are the major *political* structures which determine how society organizes *power*? E.g.:
  —procedures of decision-making
  —access to public influence
  —formal: constitution, party, courts, military
  —informal: cliques, lobbying
  —participation patterns
3. What are the major *social* structures which determine how society organizes *relationships* (other than those which are primarily economic and political relationships)? E.g.:
  —family, clan, tribe
  —neighborhood
  —education, recreation
  —communications, media
  —language patterns
4. What are the major *cultural* structures which determine how society organizes *meaning*? E.g.:
  —religion
  —symbols, myths, dreams
  —art, music, folk-lore
  —lifestyle, traditions

C. What are the key *values* operative in this structure?

We speak here of values as the goals that motivate people, the ideologies and moral norms that guide, the aspirations and expectations that people have, the social emphases that are acceptable and accepted. These are, of course, related to the cultural structures.

1. What are the "carriers" of values in society—persons, role models, institutions?
2. Examples of various sets of values:
  —life
  —age/youth
  —unity/diversity
  —individualism/community
  —competition/cooperation

—materialism/spiritualism
—accumulation/sharing
—power and influence/serving
—participation/obedience
—freedom/law and order
—progress/stability
—innovation/tradition
—justice/security
—peace/violence
—equality/hierarchy

D. What is the future *direction* of this situation?

A look into the future may in fact reveal more about the present than about the future. That is, the futuristic exercise of imagining "scenarios" gives us insights into the dynamics of what is actually occurring now.

1. What are the most significant trends revealed in the present situation?
2. What can we "extrapolate" (i.e., project by inference) from the current scene?
3. If things keep going in the future the way they are going now, what will be the situation in ten years?
4. What are the sources of creativity and hope for the future in the present situation?

IV. Conclusions

The analysis we have made will have opened up a variety and multiplicity of factors which influence the situation we are trying to understand. The final task is now to draw some conclusions, to be able to discern the most important elements in the situation. This requires that we look over the responses made to the four analytical questions and identify—by a process of ranking—the "root" elements.

"Root" elements are the most basic causes—"causal causes"—in a situation. They are distinct from symptoms or mere consequences of something deeper. In the social analysis approach offered by Paulo Freire, they are called "generative themes"; in the approach of François Houtart, they are "determinative/dominative" causes. They are the answers that finally turn up when we continually ask the question, "Why?"

To uncover these "root" elements, we first must prioritize or rank within each analytical category (history, structures, values, direction) the most significant factors influencing the situation. For example, which one or two historical events most shaped the present? Which economic, political, social, and cultural factors most determine the operation of the system? Which one or two values have the most impact on how people act? Which trend seems most likely for the future of the situation?

Struggling to answer such questions, we will feel the need to identify some criteria by which we conclude that some elements are more basic than others. Development of such criteria, of course, is a major task of social philosophy. It is also dependent on a return to experience, the experience of trial and error. In the methodology presented here, no formalized criteria are offered. Rather, a strong suggestion is made that one of the key sources for criteria will be the fundamentals made explicit in the first step, "conversion."

When the various elements have been prioritized, we need to make a second effort at ranking and then draw some conclusions.

1. **What are the two or three "root" elements most responsible for the current situation?**
2. **In whose interests do these root elements operate?**

The conclusions we can draw from such a social analytical approach will obviously depend on a variety of factors: the relative complexity of the situation we are studying, the accuracy and adequacy of the data available to us, the rigor of our questioning, the criteria which influence our own judgments on "root" elements, etc. But the advantage of doing this exercise in this way is that it does begin to open up the situation and reveal causes, consequences, linkages, trends, and related dimensions. It provides a holistic picture—dynamic in a historical perspective and interconnected in a structural perspective.

A Simpler Approach

The outline of the practical methodology presumes a fair capacity to work with analytical tools at a more or less sophisticated level. It is not necessary, of course, to be an "expert" to do social analysis. This is a point we have repeatedly made in the text of our study. Moreover, we have experienced the validity of the point in the different workshops we have shared. But to work through the various steps—using the suggested terms and distinctions—does require some experience of the social sciences, some familiarity with organized academic approaches.

Knowing the more detailed background of the methodology, however, it is possible then to make use of an approach which is "simpler" at least in terminology. This approach moves through the following ten questions (each one of which, it can be seen, has parallels in the detailed steps of methodology).

1. **What do you notice about our situation here today? What are people experiencing?**
2. **What changes have occurred in the past twenty years? What have been the most important events?**
3. **What influence does money have in our situation? Why?**
4. **Who makes the most important decisions around here? Why?**
5. **What are the most important relationships people have here? Why?**
6. **What are the most important traditions of the people? Why?**
7. **What do people want most in life? Why?**
8. **What will things be like in ten years if they keep going in the same way? Why?**
9. **What are the most important causes of the way things are today? Why?**
10. **What did you learn from all of this?**

This approach might be used very effectively with some small groups which are just beginning to explore their local social reality. Moving through these ten questions opens up a situation and stimulates the desire for more profound analysis. The simple questions, of course, are only entry points into more detailed efforts.

Positive Use

Can social analysis be used in ways which open up situations which are positive, i.e., successful or promising? This question comes about because we most frequently use the tool of analysis to gain a deep understanding of serious problems, crises, or difficulties.

It is possible, however, to take a successful achievement and study the various aspects of its reality in order to understand why it has been successful. We can learn more from a success—and how to apply those lessons to the future—by studying in a systematic fashion the history, structures, values, and direction of the achievement. The method of social analysis points to the reasons for success (in our conclusion) and can be useful in demonstrating to people that change can, in fact, come about in ways which are beneficial to people.

Theological Reflection

We have emphasized that social analysis has a close connection with theological reflection. In the "pastoral circle," the two are closely related. But we would not be true to a process of social analysis which effectively "links faith and justice" if we saw these two tasks as very distinct elements or completely separated moments. In the actual doing of analysis in a pastoral situation, the theological and the social interpenetrate each other.

First, we begin our social analysis with certain theological presuppositions. That is, we have "values" and "biases" which come from our faith, from the tradition of the Christian community, from the social teaching of the church, etc. These shape and orientate our questions. Second, we do our theological reflection with at least some implicit sociological understandings, e.g., about the structure of the church, the relationship of culture and the Word of God, etc.

The emphasis on "root metaphors" as explained in the

"Foreword" to this second edition helps us understand this interpenetration of the social and the theological. The *artistic* root metaphor, which we suggested lies at the basis of liberation theology, brings together creative strains in the understanding of both social realities and religious dimensions.

In offering some practical guidelines for social analysis in this "Afterword," we can also suggest a framework for going about some explicit steps of theological reflection. (A very good development of the background and substance of theological reflection can be found in James Hug, S.J., ed., *Tracing the Spirit: Communities, Social Action, and Theological Reflection,* New York: Paulist Press, 1983.)

This simple approach can be used by small groups in a variety of ways. The elements of scripture, questions, and prayer are all key to whatever method is followed.

1. Open up the experience or situation through the tool of social analysis and identify the "root" elements.
2. Pray for light to discern the presence of the Spirit in the midst of this situation, to hear the call, to be open to the lessons.
3. Develop some specific questions for reflection, e.g., what consequences does this situation have for building a Christian community response?
4. Read some scripture which suggests itself as relevant to the theme of the reflections; or pick some passages from some documents of the church's social teaching; e.g., the Genesis story of creation; teachings of the prophets; miracles of Jesus; Vatican II statements; etc.
5. From a prayerful reflection over the readings, ask questions about the situation, e.g.:
   a) What reinforces gospel values, social teachings, etc.?
   b) What undercuts, destroys these values and these teachings?
   c) Where is Jesus present here?
   d) What are "signs of the Kingdom" in this situation?
   e) What is *grace* in this situation, as an opening up to God?

    f) What is *sin* in this situation, as a turning from God?

    g) What does "salvation" mean in this situation?

6. Also ask questions about the scripture and the teaching, e.g.:

    a) In the "real world" is it possible to put Christian teaching into practice?

    b) Is the Christian approach the only or the best approach in this situation?

    c) What more do I need to know about the scripture and teaching?

7. Ask questions about church structure and practice, e.g.:

    a) What is the role of the church here?

    b) What is the meaning of ministry, the action of the laity, the challenge to the community?

    c) What is the place of the sacraments?

    d) What "spirituality" is appropriate here?

8. Prioritize some of the major lessons which have been learned in this exercise of reflection.

9. Practice some prayerful discernment over the lessons learned.

    a) Quietly note what have been movements of light/darkness, peace/static, encouragement/discouragement, etc.

    b) Faith-share these movements with the group.

10. Pray for strength to move into the decisions and actions which are called for by the situation which has been submitted to this social analysis and theological reflection.

Obviously, this approach is only a set of suggested steps. It is not to be followed slavishly. Nor is it to be attempted all at once. But the various elements offered here, together with other approaches, can bring forth an interpretation of the reality which goes considerably beyond—much deeper than—that offered simply by social analysis.

Questionnaire 1

Beginning Social Analysis

Beginning social analysis in a local situation can be simple. First, we must ask ourselves what we know about the various sectors of our social reality. What we already know—and what we don't know—will push us to further study. Below are several questions that may help us to determine the areas upon which to focus our attention.

I. SOCIAL

A. **What is the *demographic* character of the locality?**
    present population
    growth rate (decline/increase)
    projections toward year 2000
    present geographic concentration
    projected shifts in concentration
    urban/rural differences

B. **What is its *racial/ethnic* character?**
    European ethnic groups
    Hispanics
    Blacks
    Native Americans
    Asians
    Other

C. **What is the *cultural* character of the locality?**
    ethnic heritages of population
    character or "stamp" of the people

level of education
strength of community ties
state of the arts

D. What is the *class structure* in the locality?
underclass
low income service workers
blue collar workers
white collar workers
managerial class
super-rich

E. What are the dominant *social problems* in the area? Related to:
race
migratory labor
the aging
women
families
youth
abortion
schools
drugs; alcohol
health care
leisure activities
crime
other

F. What is the *social-psychological "temper"* of the area?
predominant values
class divisions and conflicts
general outlook on life: satisfaction/malaise

II. ECONOMIC

A. What is the general economic *profile* of the locality?
major industries
agricultural situation
natural resources
new technologies

relationship to defense/military industries
role of business and labor groups in community

B. What is the economic *situation*?
self-reliance vs. dependency
growth rate
inflation; cost of living
unemployment
income distribution
strength of unions
labor/management relations

C. What is the *environmental* situation?
pollution—air, water, land
energy prospects, present and future
effectiveness of environmental regulations

D. What are the key economic *problems*?
flight of capital
urban gentrification and displacement
housing
tax bases
public services
other

E. What is the relationship between the *local* economy and the *international* economy?
imports/exports
offices of multinational corporations
foreign-owned local businesses
runaway shops

III. POLITICAL

A. What is the political *profile* of the locality?
relationship of political parties
existence of party "machines"
liberal/conservative divisions
voting registration/election turn-out
church/state relationship

B. **What is the nature of its political *leadership*?**
record of senators/representatives in Congress
record of state legislature and governor
record of local officials

C. **What is the nature of its *informal* leadership?**
names of "influential" people
socio-economic background of leaders
connections (business, family, etc.) with other influential
    groups or individuals
nature of power concentration
active interest groups and lobbies

D. **What *non-political* factors have influence on political life?**
churches and synagogues
media
business groups
labor unions

IV. ECCLESIAL

A. **What is the *religious climate* in the locality?**
percentages of Catholics, Protestants, Jews, etc.
percentage of religiously non-affiliated
presence of religions/traditions/movements of other
    than Judeo-Christian origin
degree of ecumenical cooperation
religious affection/disaffection (provide reasons)

B. **What is the health of the *local church*?**
state of dioceses
character of bishops, church leadership
pastoral councils; participation of laity
morale/style of clergy and religious professionals
vocations (clergy, religious)
institutions—hospitals, schools, etc.

Questionnaire 2

Evaluating Social Action Responses

There is always a need for continual, honest evaluation of our actions on behalf of justice. But what sort of questions should we ask ourselves about the direction of pastoral responses to social justice challenges? Below are two sets of questions that may prove helpful in the evaluation task.

QUESTIONS ABOUT THE EFFECTIVENESS OF OUR EFFORTS

1. What is the specific need that is being addressed or that should be addressed?

2. How do our explicit religious values (e.g., the gospel message, etc.) call upon us to respond to this need?

3. How are the poor or the victims of injustice being involved in determining and defining the felt need?

4. Is social analysis being used as a tool for understanding the need in its larger context?

5. What social theories and theologies underlie the approach chosen to address the need?

6. What direct or indirect impact is being made on or by the victims of injustice?

7. What social structures, both internal and external to the group involved, are being affected by the action on behalf of justice?

8. What cooperation/collaboration with other groups (including laity and base communities) is occurring?

9. What level of "success" has been achieved in meeting the need addressed?

10. What criteria and processes have been employed to judge or measure that "success"?

11. What has happened to the people who were involved in the social justice action? Has it changed their perspectives, lifestyles, values, etc.? Has it improved various physical conditions in their lives?

12. What means have been provided for on-going social analysis?

QUESTIONS ABOUT THE VALUE OF OUR EFFORTS

1. Are *all* participants (both the "servers" and the "served") growing in self-determination and confidence?

2. Are we working *with* people, or exclusively *for* people—in planning, execution, and evaluation?

3. Are we collaborating with structures that need to be modified or changed, or are we challenging and changing them? Are we being co-opted by the forces that support those structures?

4. Is it possible to do this kind of work and *not* be co-opted?

5. Is this work becoming so rigidly institutionalized that it has lost the flexibility it needs to respond to newly emerging needs?

6. Are *all* participants in the process undergoing an expansion of consciousness about the relationship of this work to other justice issues?

7. Has this work contributed to a radical restructuring of our own group structure and lifestyle?

8. Are we making attempts to "network" with groups that have similar goals?

9. Do we perceive the needs we are addressing from both a *local* and a *global* perspective?

Annotated Bibliography

There are many resources that can help the reader enhance his or her understanding of social analysis. Listed below are some suggestions for further reading:

Peter Berger and Thomas Luckmann. *The Social Construction of Reality*. Garden City, New York: Doubleday/Anchor, 1967.
    Helpful explanation of the meaning of social structures and their role in the life of individuals and society.

Harry C. Boyte. *The Backyard Revolution: Understanding the New Citizen Movement*. Philadelphia: Temple University Press, 1980.
    Analyzes the creative communitarian social movements in the United States, and calls for the Left to root itself in populist culture, both practically and theoretically.

Mary P. Burke, *Reaching for Justice: The Women's Movement*. Washington, D.C.: CENTER OF CONCERN, 1980.
    A concise history of the women's movement and its challenge to the traditional structures of society. Examines the context out of which the movement arose and explores the questions it has raised for society and for religion.

Richard J. Cassidy. *Catholic Teaching Regarding Capitalism and Socialism*. Office of Justice and Peace, Archdiocese of Detroit, 1979.
    A good review of the development of Catholic social thought as it pertains to capitalism and socialism. Discusses the changes in the analysis, particularly the shift of the past 100 years.

Catholic Bishops of Appalachia. *This Land is Home to Me*. Prestonsburg, Kentucky: Catholic Committee on Appalachia, 1975.
An important pastoral letter of the Catholic bishops of the Appalachian region in the United States. It was the first official North American Catholic document to draw upon the Latin American style of social analysis.

Thomas Clarke, ed. *Above Every Name: The Lordship of Christ and Social Systems*. New York: Paulist Press, 1980.
Theological essays based on the understanding that the Reign of God has structural consequenses in our world today. Includes a chapter by Philip Land of Center of Concern, analyzing the economic order.

John Coleman. *An American Strategic Theology*. New York: Paulist Press, 1982.
An important effort at dialogue between theology and sociology within the specifics of the North American context. Utilizes the "pastoral circle" in several places.

Michael Czerny, ed. *Canadian Social Analysis*. Toronto: Jesuit Centre for Social Faith and Justice, 1983.
Application of church social teaching perspectives to specific Canadian issues. Helpful for those beginning the process of social analysis for justice involvement. (Available from 947 Queen St. East, Toronto M4, 1J9, Canada.)

John Derochers. *Methods of Societal Analysis*. Dasarahalli, Bangalore, India: St. Paul Press, 1977.
Reviews the historical/structural approach to analysis; types of societies; economic, political, and social systems; and the interaction of religion and culture. The context is India, but much of the discussion has wider import. (Available from Christian Institute for the Study of Religion and Society, P.O. Box 4600, Bangalore 560046, India.)

William W. Everett and T.J. Bachmeyer. *Disciplines in Transformation: A Guide to Theology and the Behavioral Sciences.* Washington, D.C.: University Press of America, 1979.
Analyzes three styles of social science, three of psychology, and three of Christianity. Argues that there is a methodological similarity between particular styles of each. A good beginning for an important methodological debate.

Harry Fagan. *Empowerment: Skills for Parish Social Action.* New York: Paulist Press, 1979.
From a practical point of view rooted in considerable experience, this study shows the various steps necessary to move people to take action in promoting changes for justice in their local areas.

Andrew M. Greeley. *No Bigger Than Necessary.* New York: New American Library, 1977.
Shows how the Catholic social tradition can be an antidote to the bureaucratization of capitalism and socialism. Rhetorically hostile to new developments in Catholic social thought, but contains valuable insights that can be assimilated by the new thrust.

Joseph Gremillion, ed. *The Gospel of Justice and Peace: Catholic Social Teaching Since Pope John.* Maryknoll, N.Y.: Orbis Books, 1976.
Contains the basic social documents of the Catholic church during the time of Pope John XXIII and Pope Paul VI, plus an excellent introduction and overview of the development of this teaching by Msgr. Gremillion.

John Haughey, ed. *The Faith That Does Justice.* New York: Paulist Press, 1977.
Written by theologians from the Woodstock Theological Center—reflections on the linkages of faith and justice in the new social context.

Peter Henriot, S.J., et al. *The Context of Our Ministries: Working Papers*. Washington: Jesuit Conference, 1981.
  A look at the U.S. scene as the context of evangelization today. Workbook prepared by a team of social scientists and theologians, based on the methodology of the "pastoral circle."

Joe Holland. *The American Journey*. New York and Washington, D.C.: IDOC and the Center of Concern, 1976.
  An overview of American history with special emphasis on the nation's social struggles and its present domestic and international crisis.

Joe Holland. *Flag, Faith and Family: Rooting the American Left in Everyday Symbols*. Chicago: New Patriotic Alliance, 1979.
  Discusses the failure of the American Left to grasp the creative role of collective symbols in the process of social change. Uses examples of flag, faith, and family (nation, religion, and kinship) to illustrate the importance of cultural symbols and the consequences of ignoring them.

James Hug, ed. *Tracing the Spirit: Communities, Social Action, and Theological Reflection*. New York: Paulist Press, 1983.
  Essays on the methodology of theological reflection, particularly in conjunction with social action for justice. Contains a chapter by Joe Holland, which explores the link between social analysis and theological reflection.

Interreligious Taskforce for Social Analysis. *Must We Choose Sides? Christian Commitment for the 1980's*. Washington, D.C., 1980.
  Includes the analyses of various authors, plus six comprehensive sessions with group exercises that incorporate the insights of experience, apply tools of analysis, and participate in theological reflection.

Interreligious Taskforce on U.S. Food Policy. *Identifying a Food Policy Agenda for the 1980's*. Washington, D.C., 1980.
  Example of social analysis of development issues. Includes the-

ological reflection on the religious vocation to respond to justice issues.

James Jennings, ed. *Economics, Values and Reality: An Educational Experience in the Use of Social Analysis.* Washington, D.C.: United States Catholic Conference, 1982.
Presents an overview of the importance of social analysis and various approaches to it, from the experience of the work of the Campaign for Human Development.

John Kavanaugh. *Following Christ in a Consumer Society.* Maryknoll, N.Y.: Orbis Books, 1981.
A profound analysis of the cultural foundations of the U.S. economic system, with implications for Christian responses.

J. B. Libanio. *Spiritual Discernment and Politics.* Maryknoll, N.Y.: Orbis Books, 1982.
Social analysis from a Latin American perspective. A Brazilian author expands the classic understanding of discernment to take account of the social context within which the discernment occurs.

Maryknoll Fathers and Brothers. *Social Analysis According to Gospel Values: A Resource Manual for Planners.* Maryknoll, N.Y.: Maryknoll Mission Research and Planning Department, 1979.
An edited collection of approaches to analyzing social/economic/political situations. Includes sample questions, evaluation materials, and a number of items useful for local application.

Maryknoll Fathers and Brothers. *Social Analysis and Research With Grassroots Groups: Basic Models and Approaches.* Maryknoll, N.Y.: Maryknoll Mission Research and Planning Department, 1981.
Helpful summary of four models for doing social analysis with local groups. Includes discussion of approaches of INODEP (Freire), CETRI (Houtart), and Ecumenical Institute.

James and Kathleen McGinnis. *Parenting for Peace and Justice*. Maryknoll, N.Y.: Orbis Books, 1982.
Shows the importance of a deeper analytical understanding of justice if education of children in family situations is to be realistically grounded.

Arthur F. McGovern. *Marxism: An American Christian Perspective*. Maryknoll, N.Y.: Orbis Books, 1980.
Clear study of Marxism and Christianity and their encounter, from both philosophical and theological points of view.

Theology in the Americas. *Is Liberation Theology for America? The Response of First World Churches*. (Available from Theology in the Americas, 475 Riverside Dr., Rm. 1268, New York, NY 10027).
Contains papers from a 1978 seminar. Theology in the Americas has been a key bridge for dialogue between Latin American liberation theology and the Christian exploration of social analysis in North America.

James Wallis. *Call to Conversion: Recovering the Gospel for These Times*. San Francisco: Harper and Row, 1981.
A challenging social spirituality from an evangelical viewpoint (Sojourners). While not specifically presenting social analysis, it highlights the critical link of faith and justice in the political and pastoral responses needed today.

Gibson Winter. *Elements for a Social Ethic: The Role of Social Science in Public Policy*. New York: Macmillan, 1966.
Philosophical reflections by an American theologian on the behaviorist, functionalist, voluntarist, and intentional perspectives in social science. Difficult reading, but a classic.

Gibson Winter. *Liberating Creation: Foundations of Religious Social Ethics*. New York: Crossroad, 1981.
An analysis of the social and spiritual crisis of the mechanistic root metaphor as the foundation of modern Western culture. Key resource for linking social analysis and theological reflection.

Center Publications Coming Soon

The American Journey, 2nd edition, by Joe Holland.
Long out of print, we have had many requests to make this book available again and bring it up to date. This new edition will contain a fresh introduction and a new chapter tracing developments since 1976 up to the Reagan years.

Church and Labor in the World Economy, by Joe Holland and Maria Riley, O.P.
A primer for church activists and trade unionists around the world. It will explain the history, structures, and tendencies in the world labor movement; review church teaching on labor; analyze the new situation of workers' movements and the new challenge from women workers; and offer an appendix on resources across the globe.

Religion and Labor in America, by Joe Holland and Steve Askin.
Growing out of the experience of the expanding "religion and labor" networks in the United States, this book will analyze the history, present struggles, and future coalition possibilities.

About the CENTER OF CONCERN . . .

The CENTER OF CONCERN, founded in 1971, is an independent, interdisciplinary team engaged in social analysis, religious reflection, policy advocacy, and public education around questions of social justice. We place particular stress on the global dimension and its importance for domestic issues. Holding consultative status with the United Nations, the CENTER has participated in many U.N. conferences on international social policy on issues of population, food, women's rights, trade, development, unemployment. The CENTER has outreach into the policy-making, religious, and civic communities, and conducts a variety of workshops and institutes on themes linking faith and justice. Our bi-monthly newsletter, CENTER FOCUS, is available free of charge. The CENTER has no assured means of income and so welcomes contributions toward its work.

 CENTER OF CONCERN
3700 13th Street, N.E.
Washington, D.C. 20017
(202) 635-2757